All Bible references taken from the KJV of the Bible, unless otherwise indicated.

<u>Churchzilla</u>, *The Self-Centered, Wanna-Be, Supposed-to-Be Bridezilla of Christ*

Cover art adapted from
ID <u>3312565</u> © <u>Madartists</u> | <u>Dreamstime.com</u>

Adapted by Dr. Marlene Miles

Freshwater Press, USA

ISBN: 978-1-960150-00-4

Paperback Version

Copyright 2022 by Dr. Marlene Miles

All rights reserved. No part of this book may be reproduced, distributed, or transmitted by any means or in any means including photocopying, recording or other electronic or mechanical methods without prior written permission of the publisher except in the case of brief publications or critical reviews.

Table of Contents

Preface	4
The Bachelor	11
The Bride of Christ	21
Bridezilla	29
Without Spot, Blemish, or Wrinkle	47
The Seven Women	50
The Crisis of False Shepherds	76
Touch Not Mine Anointed	88
Not Discerning the Body	92
Churchzillas	101
The Old Maids	108
Adorning the Bride	114
Thank God for Grace and Mercy	123
Dear Reader	128
Prayer books by this author	129
Other books by this author	130
Other Series	137

Churchzilla

The Self-Centered, Wanna-Be, Supposed-to-Be **Bridezilla** *of Christ*

Freshwater Press

Preface

And in that day, seven women shall take hold of one man saying, we will eat our own bread and wear our own apparel only let us be called by thy name to take away our reproach.   Isaiah 4:1

Seven women are lined up to win the Bachelor. He is Christ and the Seven Women are the Seven Churches of the Revelation. But how can She be His bride if she is not being *prepared?*

Isaiah prophesied that seven women would vie for one man to be married to take away society's reproach. Prophetically, seven Churches vie to marry the Lamb of God. Each has to be made ready by proper teaching, preaching and leadership.

Revelations 2:1 to 4:1, *(emphasis added, mine.)*

Unto the angel of the church of Ephesus write, These things saith he that holdeth the seven stars in his right hand, who walketh in the midst of the seven golden candlesticks;

I know thy works, and thy labour, and thy patience, and how thou canst not bear them which are evil: and thou hast tried them which say they are apostles, and are not, and hast found them liars:

And hast borne, and hast patience, and for my name's sake hast laboured, and hast not fainted.

Nevertheless I have somewhat against thee, because thou hast left thy first love.

Remember therefore from whence thou art fallen, and repent, and do the first works; or else I will come unto thee quickly, and will remove thy candlestick out of his place, except thou repent.

But this thou hast, that thou hatest the deeds of the Nicolaitanes, which I also hate.

He that hath an ear, let him hear what the Spirit saith unto the churches; To him that overcometh will I give to eat of the tree of life, which is in the midst of the paradise of God.

And unto the angel of the church in Smyrna write; These things saith the first and the last, which was dead, and is alive;

I know thy works, and tribulation, and poverty, (but thou art rich) and I know the blasphemy of them which say they are Jews, and are not, but are the synagogue of Satan.

Fear none of those things which thou shalt suffer: behold, the devil shall cast some of you into prison, that ye may be tried; and ye shall have tribulation ten days: be thou faithful unto death, and I will give thee a crown of life.

He that hath an ear, let him hear what the Spirit saith unto the churches; He that overcometh shall not be hurt of the second death.

And to the angel of the church in Pergamos write; These things saith he which hath the sharp sword with two edges;

I know thy works, and where thou dwellest, even where Satan's seat is: and thou holdest fast my name, and hast not denied my faith, even in those days wherein Antipas was my faithful martyr, who was slain among you, where Satan dwelleth.

But I have a few things against thee, because thou hast there them that hold the doctrine of Balaam, who taught Balac to cast a stumblingblock before the children of Israel, to eat things sacrificed unto idols, and to commit fornication.

So hast thou also them that hold the doctrine of the Nicolaitanes, which thing I hate.

Repent; or else I will come unto thee quickly and will fight against them with the sword of my mouth.

He that hath an ear, let him hear what the Spirit saith unto the churches; To him that overcometh will I give to eat of the hidden manna, and will give him a white stone, and in the stone a new name written, which no man knoweth saving he that receiveth it.

And unto the angel of the church in Thyatira write; These things saith the Son of God, who hath his eyes like unto a flame of fire, and his feet are like fine brass;

I know thy works, and charity, and service, and faith, and thy patience, and thy works; and the last to be more than the first.

Notwithstanding I have a few things against thee, because thou sufferest that woman Jezebel, which calleth herself a prophetess, to teach and to seduce my servants to commit fornication, and to eat things sacrificed unto idols.

And I gave her space to repent of her fornication; and she repented not.

Behold, I will cast her into a bed, and them that commit adultery with her into great tribulation, except they repent of their deeds.

And I will kill her children with death; and all the churches shall know that I am he which searcheth the reins and hearts: and I will give unto every one of you according to your works.

But unto you I say, and unto the rest in Thyatira, as many as have not this doctrine, and which have not known the depths of Satan, as they speak; I will put upon you none other burden.

But that which ye have already hold fast till I come.

And he that overcometh, and keepeth my works unto the end, to him will I give power over the nations:

And he shall rule them with a rod of iron; as the vessels of a potter shall they be broken to shivers: even as I received of my Father.

And I will give him the morning star.

He that hath an ear, let him hear what the Spirit saith unto the churches.

And unto the angel of the church in Sardis write; These things saith he that hath the seven Spirits of God, and the seven stars; I know thy works, that thou hast a name that thou livest, and art dead.

Be watchful, and strengthen the things which remain, that are ready to die: for I have not found thy works perfect before God.

Remember therefore how thou hast received and heard, and hold fast, and repent. If therefore thou shalt not watch, I will come on thee as a thief, and thou shalt not know what hour I will come upon thee.

Thou hast a few names even in Sardis which have not defiled their garments; and they shall walk with me in white: for they are worthy.

He that overcometh, the same shall be clothed in white raiment; and I will not blot out his name out of the book of life, but I will confess his name before my Father, and before his angels.

He that hath an ear, let him hear what the Spirit saith unto the churches.

And to the angel of the church in Philadelphia write; These things saith he that is holy, he that is true, he that hath the key of David, he that openeth, and no man shutteth; and shutteth, and no man openeth;

I know thy works: behold, I have set before thee an open door, and no man can shut it: for thou hast a little strength, and hast kept my word, and hast not denied my name.

Behold, I will make them of the synagogue of Satan, which say they are Jews, and are not, but do lie; behold, I will make them to come and worship before thy feet, and to know that I have loved thee.

Because thou hast kept the word of my patience, I also will keep thee from the hour of temptation, which shall come upon all the world, to try them that dwell upon the earth.

Behold, I come quickly: hold that fast which thou hast, that no man take thy crown.

Him that overcometh will I make a pillar in the temple of my God, and he shall go no more out: and I will write upon him the name of my God, and the name of the city of my God, which is new Jerusalem, which cometh down out of heaven from my God: and I will write upon him my new name.

He that hath an ear, let him hear what the Spirit saith unto the churches.

And unto the angel of the church of the Laodiceans write; These things saith the Amen, the faithful and true witness, the beginning of the creation of God;

I know thy works, that thou art neither cold nor hot: I would thou wert cold or hot.

So then because thou art lukewarm, and neither cold nor hot, I will spue thee out of my mouth.

Because thou sayest, I am rich, and increased with goods, and have need of nothing; and knowest not that thou art wretched, and miserable, and poor, and blind, and naked:

I counsel thee to buy of me gold tried in the fire, that thou mayest be rich; and white raiment, that thou mayest be clothed, and that the shame of thy nakedness do not appear; and anoint thine eyes with eyesalve, that thou mayest see.

As many as I love, I rebuke and chasten: be zealous therefore, and repent.

Behold, I stand at the door, and knock: if any man hear my voice, and open the door, I will come in to him, and will sup with him, and he with me.

To him that overcometh will I grant to sit with me in my throne, even as I also overcame, and am set down with my Father in his throne.

He that hath an ear, let him hear what the Spirit saith unto the churches.

After this I looked, and, behold, a door was opened in heaven: and the first voice which I heard was as it were of a trumpet talking with me; which said, Come up hither, and I will shew thee things which must be

Which is as a bridegroom coming out of his chamber, and rejoiceth as a strong man to run a race.(Psalm 19:5)

The Bachelor

Let's meet our Bachelor. He is the oldest in His family, being the first born of many brethren. He is well traveled. He was born in Bethlehem, Israel, but He's traveled far and wide as an ambassador of sorts, about His Father's business. He's been places that no one else has ever gone. He is well read, well versed and always knows what to say in any given situation. He is altogether lovely. He is comely, good looking, and very handsome. He is fine. His countenance shines like the sun. He is the Daystar, the Bright and Morning Star. He is the Rose of Sharon and the Lily of the Valley. He is *all that*. He is Alpha and Omega, the First and the Last. His disposition is good. He is slow to wrath--, usually. He is sweeter than the honey in a honeycomb. He is adorable and irresistible.

He is your Ever-Present Help in times of trouble. He is for you; He is always on your side. He is your Advocate. He is your Comfort. He will wipe away all your tears.

He is pure of heart. There's no guile in Him. He is a Peacemaker. He is a Prince, He *is* Peace. He is the Prince of Peace. He is the Prince of Life. He is your Counselor, your Friend.

He is a child of God. He is meek and lowly, but He is no pushover. He is a Lamb, but He is also a Lion.

His mind is ever on you. He is thoughtful. He comes bringing gifts, wonderful, and amazing gifts. He is Wonderful. He is Faithful. He is ever bragging on you.

He rightly divides, judging with Mercy and Truth. He is well balanced. He hates a false balance. He's kind, compassionate and gentle. He speaks in a still small voice. He is not puffed up or boisterous. He is patient and longsuffering. He doesn't insist on His own way. He is a gentleman. He doesn't think on evil, and it's not easily provoked. He doesn't misbehave or behave Himself in an inappropriate way. He will not embarrass you in public or bring you to shame. He celebrates Truth, not those things that are wrong. He *is* Truth. He bears, hopes, endures, and believes all things. He never fails. He is Love. He is meek. God-like. He is faithful. He is joy. He is peaceful and temperate.

A faithful man, *who can find*? He is Faithful. He is not a man that He should lie, nor the son of man, that He should repent.

He's good like His Father. He is good all the time.

He is forgiving. He doesn't hold grudges. Every morning, new mercies. He will redeem you from your debts. He is, as your Boaz, the Kinsman Redeemer. He will pull you out of the miry clay and establish you. He will lift you out of many waters and set your feet in a large, green place. In a dry and thirsty land where no water is, He will lead you to the Rock that is higher.

He is your Redeemer. He will step in and take your place when things are too hard. He is your propitiation, your Substitute. His yoke is easy, and His burden is light.

He's very rich. All the silver and the gold belong to Him. All the cattle on 1000 hills are His. The Earth is His, and the fullness thereof.

He is a master teacher, *Rabboni*. He imparts Wisdom, giving it liberally to those who ask in faith because He would not have you ignorant. He's really smart, wise, and intelligent. People want to think just like Him –, let this mind be in you that was also in Christ Jesus.

He helps you grow up and mature.

He is a shield, a buckler, and a strong tower that the righteous can run into and they are safe. He is a warrior; the Lord is His name. He is our Banner. He will fight your battles for you. He will contend with those who contend with you. He is mighty; He is the King of Glory. He is the Lion of the Tribe of Judah, and when He roars you will know it. He will defend you from your enemies and He will defend your honor. He won't let people walk all over you. He is strong. Power belongs to Him, and all honor, and all glory.

He will protect you.

He is majestic; Majesty belongs to Him. He is all glorious. Strength belongs to Him.

He is the Perfect Man, the perfect husband-to-be. He will protect the authority you have as a *wife*. He will walk in His own authority and maintain divine order in the home. He will beat down the enemies of your soul. Shouts of victory and joy are heard in His camp.

He's on your side. He will bless those that bless you.

He is **_the_** man, in a good way, the Perfect Man.

He is organized, He does all things decently and in order. You'll never have to pick up His socks or clean up after Him. Nothing profane comes out of His mouth; He is decent, and all of His ways are pure, clean, Righteous and Holy.

He is giving. He *first* gives and He keeps on giving. He gave gifts unto men. He will rebuke the devourer for your sake. He will cause your enemies to flee from you seven ways. He prospers you in your checking and savings accounts and your harvest will always be plentiful. Whether in the city or the country, with Him, you will be blessed, because of Him. Everything you set your hands to will prosper. He is your ultimate Provider, supplying all things according to His riches and glory.

He *first* loves you, even if you don't love Him first. There is no risk.

He's a chip off the old block. The fruit did not fall far from the tree. He only says what He hears His Father say. He only does what He sees His Father do. He is a family man, a vine with deep roots and family ties. He loves children, He wants children. He wants you to bring them forth. He wants you to be fruitful and multiply.

He is friendly and shows Himself friendly, and He sticks closer than a brother.

He is your Shepherd. Would you enjoy a lovely picnic? He will lead you by still waters and into green pastures. He will prepare a table before you even in the presence of your enemies, but you do not have to fear. His banner over you is Love.

He is all about His work. He is obedient and diligent to do everything His Father gives Him to do. Yet He is ever present.

He is Light. He is the Bread of Heaven, giving bread to the eater and seed to the Sower. He is a miracle worker. He is a Healer. If your eyes are blind, He can open them. If your ears are deaf, He can heal them. The lame will leap, and the dumb will speak. He can bind up your heart if it is broken, He can restore your emotions, renew your mind, and create in you a clean heart. He can restore your soul.

He opened the prison doors to set the captives free.

He is attentive, never leaving, or forsaking you yet, forsaking all others for His bride.

He can fix things. He can build things. He was trained as a carpenter. He can make something out of nothing.

He has tremendous oratory and communication skills. He is an active listener; He hears and remembers everything you say. He serves God, He doesn't murmur or complain, but if you do, He will still listen. He is full of Grace and Wisdom and Truth.

He is alive. He is the Only Living God.

He is glorious but He is not arrogant; instead, He is humble. He is the Right Hand of God.

And talk about forever. His forever is Eternal. He doesn't believe in divorce. He is a covenant-maker and a covenant-keeper. You will never have a problem with commitment with Him. He will never leave you.

He is the total package. He is perfect. He is the Perfect Man. He is the **Bachelor**.

Because He is the *Bachelor*, there will be women vying for His favor. As this is really not a dating *game*, then all seriousness should prevail as the women who desire His favor need to prepare, and then present themselves for consideration and betrothal to the **Bachelor**.

Confirmed bachelors are numerous in our society and culture. These *bachelors* range from the selfishly noncommittal, to the genuinely hurt who can't get past their unhealed hurts, unresolved issues, and disappointments, to those who are perpetrating scams and are on the down low. Some are misogynists who have not learned to love women. People who don't love women do not know how to love; yet all their mothers were women.

Our Bachelor is **not** a *confirmed* bachelor. He **chooses** to be married. He's not on the down low. He is not selfish. Neither is He noncommittal. He is not hurt and embittered, He is not a stuck and emotional cripple, who is stuck in his emotional past. There is nothing *wilderness* about out Bachelor. He is prepared, ready and <u>expecting</u> to be married, and His Father has arranged the very same for Him at a prophetic future time.

There's not to be a shotgun wedding. At least it is not to be for the Lord. He **wants** to be married; He wants a wife. Will the Bride have to be *forced* to marry? That is a whole other consideration. But as for the Bachelor, just as OT patriarchs sent for wives for their sons, their heirs, so is the Bachelor's Father also looking for His Son's Beloved. And the Son is prepared for marriage.

As the woman came from the first man, Adam, she must now return to the second Adam. God always begins with the end in mind. This Bachelor is not being forced into marriage. However, for the bride, perhaps it is a different story because it seems that the Women (Churches) who are to vie for His hand seem reticent to prepare. Are they frivolous? Lazy? Disorganized? Or are they distracted by all the cares of this world, perhaps even *entangled* in those cares--, even to *disobedience*? We wonder, and in this book, we will look to see what preparation has taken place.

Abraham sent servants to choose the bride for Isaac, the Bachelor's Father has chosen a Bride for Him from the first chosen people group, from the House of Israel, and then the grafting-in of the wild ones, the Gentiles. The Bride is the *ecclesia,* the called-out ones, the Bride is the Church.

The only ways one can get into a family is to be born into it, be adopted or *marry* into it. God wants us in the family, His Family. Therefore, the Church is the prophetic Bride of Christ. We've accepted the Blood of Jesus for our salvation, but marriage is necessary. Marriage is a blood covenant. In this case it is the blood covenant that puts the woman back where she came from, back with the man, to make the whole.

Regarding marriage, according to Jewish custom, the betrothal is made, then the man goes away; both he and the bride to *prepare* themselves. No man knows the day or the hour of His return, not even the bride. It is the same for us. None of us know the exact day or hour of the soon coming of the Lord Jesus Christ to receive His Bride unto Himself. Jesus has gone to prepare a place for us so that where He is we may be also.

The Bachelor will choose His bride from the called-out ones, the Church.

Many are called, but few are chosen,
(Matthew 20:16).

If He chooses you, there will never be a dull moment. He is adventurous and exciting. He will take you places you never thought you'd go--, higher heights than you ever imagined, and He will give you hinds feet for your high places. There may be some low places as He Himself has ascended, but He first descended; you may have to do the same. He can make your crooked places straight, and your waste places flowing water springs.

He takes the time to know you. He knows you better than you know yourself. Yet He will be better to you than you are to yourself. He knows what real love is. His Father has given Him love to give you and He will give you that love patiently and consistently, always, and forever, Jesus.

*Come hither and I will show the bride, the Lamb's wife (*Revelations 21:9b)

The Bride of Christ

Come close and I will show you the bride, the Lamb's *intended*. The brides-to-be are like Cinderella's stepsisters who each imagine that she will marry the Prince. The stepsisters each believed and hoped that the glass slipper would fit her. Little thought may have been given to the fact that a glass slipper is very hard and uncomfortable and feet that are forced into them will hurt and sweat because glass doesn't allow the foot to breathe. Less thought to the fact that next to no work could be done in a brittle shoe that might shatter if too much force is applied. No thought to the potential pain and injury of a shattered shoe that could cut, maim, or inflame the wearer. Even if the shoe fits the wearer of said glass slippers, assuming the matching pair, must tread softly and gently. She cannot kick up a ruckus, neither can she do anything too strenuous that would not become a Princess, nor doing anything that would be considered improper or inappropriate. But I'm sure the Prince and His Father have already thought this through.

But has the bride thought it through? Each of Cinderella's stepsisters was willing to *pretend* to be something that she wasn't to get a payday that would bring her honor, attention, notoriety, position, power, and the *good life,* no worries for retirement, and a husband to take away her reproach, you know, the shame of not having a husband--, the shame of being single. However, without the shoe being designed and made for a person, especially made of glass, which has no *give* whatsoever, an impostor could never fit the shoe.

Why then would a hopeful potential bride *pretend* to be something to win the groom? And in the case of Christ, *could she?*

The Bride of Christ must fit into a shoe of sorts. She must be able to follow in the footprints of Christ, following appointed Christian leaders as they follow Christ. She must be sober, hospitable, able to teach. She must be mature, not tossed to and fro by winds of doctrine. She must be intimate with the Lord, worship and rightly divide the Word of Truth and be able to give an answer for what She believes. She must exemplify love and be prepared to be a helpmate. She must be above reproach, without spot, blemish, or wrinkle. I believe that shoe is a width AA or narrower because broad is the way that leads to destruction and narrow is the way that leads to eternal life.

That shoe might be a sized A plus because Jesus had a more excellent ministry.

As with glasshouses, no stones should or could be thrown at that shoe. That shoe and the one who fits it and wears it must be above reproach.

That shoe must *be* The Gospel of the Preparation of Peace.

There are many characteristics of the prophetic Bride of Christ, and we will discuss them as this treatise evolves. But certainly God, who looks on the heart cannot be fooled. The Bride could look like a bride in the natural to the natural eye, but God judges the inward things. God is not mocked. People judge the outward, but the Lord sees the heart. You can't trick God, there's no mystery or revelation, really, since it's written in the Bible. But will there be a surprise to those folks who think they're smarter than everyone else? Better than most and wiser, slicker. Trickier? Will it be a surprise to those brides who, like foolish, undisciplined students who cram for exams and somehow pass? They believe that they can *cram* their preparation to be married into a month, week, day or hour.

Absurd; they don't even know *when* Christ is returning. Will it be a surprise to them when they find out that even if they fool folks all their life, they can't fool Christ? If they're not ready, they're just not ready. The church is designated as the Bride of Christ. She has to be prepared to come before the Lord without spot, blemish, wrinkle or any such thing.

Abraham sent his servant with jewelry to obtain a wife for his son Isaac. God sent His servant to obtain a bride for His Son, Jesus. Can His servant, be a servant and a son? Yes, aren't you? Can a son be a son and a servant also? Yes. Aren't you? The Bride (Church) was also sent by the Father.

Christ came for and is returning for His Bride.

While She is in the Earth, the Bride is to be in preparation for the Lamb. The Church is to be organized, unified, fitly joined together, matured, growing in Grace, Wisdom and understanding, wanting for no good thing. This is His bride, His beloved. She's sealed with the earnest until the day of redemption, by the Holy Spirit.

She should be glorious, adorned on the inside with a meek and teachable spirit. She shall be prepared on the outside. Yes, with preparations such as Esther was for about a year before she was presented to King Xerxes. But obedience, diligence, faithfulness, good works prepare her to show forth, love, and kindness.

Obeying the great commandment to love one another and to do the work of an evangelist, preaching the gospel to all people groups to the uttermost parts of the Earth.

The Church prophesies the triumphant return of our Lord Jesus Christ, coming for His Bride. The Bride is not a harlot. She is not a paramour. She cannot date. She is betrothed to the Bachelor. No man can touch her intimately as Ham saw Noah's nakedness, no man can see Christ's Bride intimately. The Glorious Bride of Christ, no man should look on Her with covetousness or lust. No man should abuse Her. No man should try to harness Her authority, power, influence, or wealth for his own purposes. No man, no woman, no one. She is God's.

She is to be pure, a virgin, as it were.

In the Parable of the Virgins, ten virgins were to trim their lamps while waiting for the bridegroom. Five did, five did not. Those who did were prepared to *enter into* marriage with the groom. Five did not; they weren't prepared for anything. What could keep virgins, assuming they actually have oil, from trimming their lamps? Distraction? Disobedience? Ignorance? It's not as if they had a husband or kids to attend to; they were not married. The Word says that those who are married seek how they can please their husbands, but those who are single seek to please the Lord. It is not as though any of these ten had boyfriends--, they're virgins.

Lack of knowledge may have kept the virgins from trimming their lamps. Perhaps they did not know *how* to do it. Maybe they didn't have a leader or teacher. How can they learn except that a teacher teaches them? How can they be taught unless a teacher or preacher is sent to them? Perhaps they didn't have a father or mother to instruct them on the ways of preparing themselves for life, including marriage. Rick Warren states in **The Purpose Driven Life** that it all starts with God. You won't find your purpose by looking within yourself. Ten virgins, I think, were ten teenagers who, without proper guidance, only knew how to think of themselves.

Maybe they were taught, but we're simply hardheaded. Maybe they didn't know they were supposed to be getting married. Maybe they didn't *want* to get married. Maybe they were independent or selfish and didn't want to have to do what a *man (husband)* told them to do. Maybe they didn't know that they *needed* to get married because they could not redeem themselves from their own debt, not just financial debt, but spiritual (sin) debt. Maybe they were too foolish to realize that they needed to be married because it was and is the purpose and plan of God. Many are the plans in a man's heart, but it is the Lord's counsel that will stand.

Perhaps they didn't know their purpose. Their purpose was to trim their lamps. That was it, that was their sole purpose. Why didn't they? Was it laziness? Was it procrastination, which is really rebellion in slow motion. According to John Barry, *"Faith and obedience are inseparable because obedience is evidence of true faith."* Further, he adds, *"Partial obedience is not obedience at all in the eyes of God."*

Half of the ten virgins were prepared, 50% the Glorious Church at *only 50%?* Fifty percent is not glorious, half of them trimming their lamps, half being prepared, or even all of them being *half*-prepared does not exemplify a glorious church.

If a baseball player bats 500, we consider that very good. But anything less than 100% in God's world is not excellent. Jesus, Himself had a more excellent ministry, A+, 100%. If Jesus had played baseball, He would have batted 1000 and He would have batted everyone ***in***. He would have had no errors, because Jesus doesn't make mistakes. And He would have won every game, because He is not willing that even *one* would be lost.

Unbelief? Could unbelief be the reason why the virgins didn't trim their lamps? Did they believe that Jesus existed? Did they believe that He was really coming back? Prophetess Sandi Burris, author of, **Unveiling Unbelief**, states, *"One thing holding back ministries, hindering families, and affecting worship,* *one thing at the root of your inability to press in and finish the race to which God has called you-, that one thing is unbelief."* Are these virgins Doubting Thomases?

Two will be in the field and one will be taken, the other will be left. Faith without works is dead. According to your faith, it shall be unto you. If you believe that God IS, He will manifest Himself to you. If you do not, then He won't. As many as **believed**, they are the Sons of God.

How can they hear except the preacher preaches? Yet it is incumbent upon the hearer to do and obey. To not do what one knows to do is sin.

As the jewel of gold and a swine snout, so is a fair woman, which is without discretion, (Proverbs 11:22).

Bridezilla

Bridezilla is the coined word to describe a difficult, unpleasant, perfectionist bride. She leaves aggravated family, friends, and bridal vendors in her wake. (And it is also the name of a reality show about these difficult women.) She has been proposed to and is betrothed to the groom, but not yet married. It is understood, it is a well-known fact that she is getting married, so she doesn't have to violently assert that--, but she does. The ring has been accepted and more often than not, the wedding invitations have gone out. She is obsessed with her wedding as *her* perfect day and disregards the feelings of other family, bridesmaids and even the groom. Because she aspires to the perfect wedding, she is obsessed with the dress, her nails, her hair, her makeup, the church, the banquet hall, the cake, the caterer, the flowers, the decorations, and everything else. This can even spill over into control mode, where she tries to control the **size** of her bridesmaids and every other detail of this *perfect day*. I have seen some Bridezillas put their bridesmaids on diets but still kick them out of the wedding at the last minute if they haven't lost the desired amount of weight. It doesn't matter if the bridesmaid is her sister, cousin, or best friend. I've seen Bridezillas fire the wedding planner because they want to directly control the entire event. In other words, Bridezilla is a flesh creature who becomes entangled in and ladened with the *image* of things of this world. All the while, the spiritual event of covenant making is an afterthought, if that. Ironically, she puts on a white dress to symbolize purity and behaves demonically. She is a *Bridezilla*.

Like Bridezilla, in certain ways, today's church has become infatuated with Herself ---, with the process of **having church** and with Her own glory, whether God-given or self-actualized. She is entangled with the building, the adornments, the numbers who come, the numbers who give, and what numbers they give in the offerings. There's the thousand-dollar line and the hundred-dollar line at the altar. She may be seriously distracted by the CDs and record deals, the recording studio, the projects, the notoriety, the success, the TV show, the book sales, ministry invitations to come preach, sing, or dance. Oh the celebrity, the status, the success, the money--!

The Church has become an extremely self-centered and self-absorbed bride-to-be. She has become a *church*zilla. **Churchzilla** is my coined word to describe a, many times, difficult, unpleasant, perfectionist, arrogant church who most often is lacking in the things of God. She's found leaving aggravated and hurt, disappointed members, leaving friends, family, and also strangers and unbelievers in her wake. I've been married and I've been single. As a single woman I am not made welcome in many churches, but with a husband, oh yeah – *Come on in*! The same thing happens at Best Buy, but that's a store for goodness' sake.

It's all about her; she's ***Churchzilla***.

She is competitive, competing with other churches *and* denominations. Churchzilla pastors seem to be in competition with other pastors. If the presiding pastor of a Churchzilla church didn't *cause* the phenomenon, he didn't do anything to stop it, if he came in after Churchzilla was already created. So, the Churchzilla phenomenon is perpetuated, and may get worse.

Most often those trapped in the aforementioned trappings are led by non-preaching, non-servant leaders, but instead by the preacher who is building, or trying to build his own Kingdom or dynasty. Again, I am not talking about *all*, but there are enough out there that those who want to find an excuse not to come to church, not to serve the Lord, not to give in the offerings, can easily find one or two self-serving "preachers" who are bringing reproach on the name of the Lord, and upon the Church as a whole.

Before going to any church, see **what's coming out of it**, or what has come out of that church. *You shall know them by their fruit.* Check on the "fruit" from that congregation. Look at the natural children of the leaders. Are they spoiled brats? Are they put in positions where they are not even *called* and those who are called, who are not relatives, endure the Pew for years and years? If the children of the preacher are not being properly raised, how will there be any upbringing for the Body of that local congregation?

Jesus.

Of course, Jesus. Surely, but would Jesus bypass the preacher's kids to correctly rear the rest of His Church? How could He do that since the *anointing* flows from the head?

Now look at the *spiritual* children of that house. Have they matriculated? Are they in ministry or have they been sitting on the Pew for the past 40 years, waiting on the Rapture? How are they living? Are they living Christian lives, or are they CME members, (Christmas Mother's Day, and Easter)? Are they on the church role in name only, but their hearts are far away from God and from the house and things of God, or are they on fire for the LORD?

Self-Exaltation is a real problem for any and all of us, but in the Book of the Revelation, Chapter 2, the 24 Elders cast down their crowns before the King of Kings. They didn't frame their crowns in shadow boxes and build museums around them to extol their own glory. They didn't go to the jeweler to make a tiny replica of their crown into a huge ring or medallion to hang on a thick gold rope. Haman asked, in the Book of Esther, *"Who better for the king to honor than me?",* and that is vain pride. Haman also exhibited hateful pride when he planned to annihilate all the Jews because Mordecai wouldn't bow to him. Vain pride plus hateful pride equals the fullness of pride. Haman had the fullness.

Some Churchzillas have vain pride, some have hateful pride, some have both. There are degrees, but it is all sin.

Just as Bridezilla is the self-absorbed, engaged woman who is planning a marriage, Churchzilla is an engaged "woman" who's full of Herself and she is slated to be the Bride of Christ.

Psychiatrists have named a certain condition *Acquired Situational Narcissism*. **Churchzilla**, like **Bridezilla** has this disorder. This type of narcissism develops in late adolescence or early adulthood. It may be brought on by wealth, fame, and other trappings of celebrity. Teenagers and young adults today call it *celebrity status*. I'll call it **entitlement**. Things that feed the flesh make a person prideful and turns them into monsters such as Bridezilla and Churchzilla. Churches may enjoy large offerings, generous benefactors, hit CDs, notoriety, celebrity pastors, award winning, record-recording musicians, singers, and choirs. Any and all of these things can lead to a prideful church. The church that is totally debt free, the church that is rich, may fall into pride. The church that does great humanitarian deeds, the church that is famous, that famous people come to, such as politicians, movie stars, and rich sports figures could easily become narcissistic. *We've got the best worship in our church* is a statement that stems from pride or may lead to pride. *Such and such is a member here,* is another prideful statement.

A church may not enjoy any of the aforementioned celebrity status. They may just want to be famous. This also makes that church into a *Churchzilla*.

Christ said to Peter, **"Upon this rock, I will build my Church."** Jesus meant that on the revelation that Jesus is the Son of God, upon this rock of revelation, He would build His church. It would not be built on *celebrity status, who's who,* or titles.

Christ's Church had humble beginnings. I've seen for myself, cellars, and clandestine rooms in houses in Rome, for instance, and also in Paris, where church was held in secret because of the 1st century of

Christianity, one could be killed for that confession. The Apostles went from house to house preaching, teaching, baptizing, ministering the Holy Spirit, and sharing the Good News. Love for Christ was genuine and conversion, I believe was the norm, not the exception. The first Church was humble. But She was genuine. She probably wasn't timid because after that the Holy Ghost had fully come at Pentecost, there was a boldness released on the people of God. I believe She was sincere in loving Christ, and willing to risk death for what She believed in. She was passionate. She treated others with a new and the greatest Commandment, to love your neighbor as yourself. She spoke often of the ones She loved and not as much about Herself. She shared among Her members having all things in common, there was community, *Koinonia*.

Likewise, individually, when a soul is first born again, he is humbled. He is pure, he loves everyone and wants everyone saved. He will do anything for anybody. He fully realizes that and totally remembers what a wretch he is, or just recently was. His passion meter is probably off the charts. He loves everybody.

As the newly born-again soul grows and matures, perhaps as a natural toddler might do, or certainly as many teenagers do, she may pull away from her father's hand because she wants to *do it all by herself*. As she begins to feel independent of the Lord because of *lift*, which is the natural bettering of circumstances and situations for people who accept Salvation and begin to walk in the things of God, She might forget where She came from and Who brought Her out. God blesses us, but She may forget where She came from or that She didn't do this without a great deal of help. She believes Herself independent, and that She is doing it herself. As a Church, She is proud of Her building. She is proud of Her name. She is proud of how rich Her people have become. She is proud that they don't need anybody else. She is proud of the successes and notoriety of Her pastor. He's famous. He's world renowned, now. If he's not, then the local body that supports him believes that he should be. She, as the Church might feel this way, reflecting how many or most individuals might be feeling in that congregation.

The Church is proud of the size of Her auditorium and how it fills up every week. She is proud of the other amenities of the building. She might even be proud of how much it costs. She is proud of how many tune into Her broadcast. She is proud of the book and tape sales.

The Church has been taught prosperity, to the max. She probably is on prosperity overload. In the Old Testament, prosperity was a sign of God's favor on a person, community, city, or nation. Yes, prosperity is a sign, but the Lord says that *signs* are for unbelievers and that those who say they **believe** should not always look for a ***sign***.

While unsaved we are all under the Curse of the Law, which is eternal death, poverty, and sickness. When we accept Salvation, we are redeemed from the Curse of the Law. Therefore, poverty should lift or abate in our lives. This is both automatic, and at the same time it is also a process. It takes varying amounts of time, but I ask, isn't it better to be redeemed from eternal death and damnation than to have money in the bank? I especially ask this because money in the bank can't get you into Heaven, but being redeemed from eternal damnation, which does get one into Heaven, brings along with it, money in the bank. That money in the bank should vary from what you need to operate successfully with all sufficiency is given by Jehovah Jireh, our Provider all the way to *more than enough*, given by El Shaddai, by God, Who Is More Than Enough.

In Christ, there is no reason not to be both redeemed from eternal damnation ***and*** to have money in the bank. All things, decently and in order.

The Church has been taught prosperity, sometimes without balance. I first heard the Prosperity Message through my television set about 20 years ago. It usually involved the sending of money to the television preacher so that God could bless *you*. What else? What else did I have to *do* to become prosperous?

The preacher never did say. It's a good thing I didn't have any money then to send in because I would have been doing one thing out of balance and perhaps not getting the man-promised return of what that man said *God* would do, and this might have caused me to doubt God. Of course, this television preacher was not my *pastor*. And I should not have been following his voice anyway, as the Word says, *My sheep know my voice and the voice of another, they will not follow.*

The comforts of this Earth have made many *fat*, and the measure of many preachers and their congregations is how fat, how comfortable, and luxuriously their **pastor** lives. If they themselves cannot also live *fat (an indulgent lifestyle),* at least they have someone to look up to. She, the Church has been taught prosperity out of balance, and that's helped turn Her into Churchzilla.

Dr. Myles Munroe teaches eloquently from the Book of Philippians, *"My God shall supply all my needs according to his riches and glory."* Then he says, *"That comes out of Chapter 4, and the balance is that if you don't do the things in Chapters 1 through 3, you can just forget about the precious promises in Chapter 4."*

The Church has been inundated with prosperity so much that She sometimes tries to *look* the part without having the necessary foundation to **be** what She *looks* like, wants to look like, or think She looks like. Children, teenagers, the childish, and immature do the same thing. She may have buildings that She can't pay for, She has too much staff or staff with too many perks that She can't afford. She looks good. She may have had a television, radio, or Internet broadcast, but no one is supporting it except the local members. It looks good to have these things and to be able to *say* that she has these things.

The Church has also been overloaded with Grace to the exclusion of Truth. Truth? Yeah, the Laws of God. We have been bombarded with the fact that the Law is of the Old Testament, but we are in the dispensation that correlates with the New Testament. Notwithstanding, Jesus said, ***"I have not come to do away with the Law, but to fulfill it."*** Therefore, the Old Testament, the Law is imperative for the New Testament to stand. The Law cannot be discarded.

The Lord has given me an example of a young man who may have been in sin. This young man is given a brick of Truth. It is heavy, but it is Truth, and he needs it. In the course of this Truth being given, the man is **not** given Grace to balance it, just Truth. Throughout his life, he walks about here and there, heavy laden with this Truth. He carries it everywhere he goes. It is on his mind. It weighs him down. The same is true of you if you were carrying a Brick of Truth. If it were a natural brick you might carry it with your left arm. After a time that left arm will bulk up from resistance of the brick and inversely the right arm might atrophy. Any person with this problem could become lopsided. One may bulk up so much from the Truth that all he knows then is to speak Truth to people, while offering no Grace, because he *has* no Grace. This is not good because it scares people away from the Gospel.

However, when this man, who is given the Brick of Truth to carry with his left arm is also given Grace to carry in his right arm will *increase* in the natural because of the value and resistance of **_both_**. He will not become lopsided, nor will he become calloused or hardened. Jesus was the Truth, **and** He was full of Grace. The OT is the Law, the NT is Grace. As we all know, the OT is larger than the NT by volume, by chapters and pages. The OT is 39 Books, at 1184 pages, while the NT is 27 Books, (421 pages). Is the Law, **weightier** than the NT, *spiritually*? I'd say no, because God is a God of justice and balance, so they are equal no matter how the sizes or volumes appear.

Randy Alcorn states that Jesus was so full of Grace that people wanted to be around Him so much that they tore roofs off of buildings to let their lame in.

It's as though today's Church is saying, *"Preach to me. Make me feel good. Preach prosperity, but don't tell me anything about obedience, tithing, giving, loving, getting along with folks, or winning the lost. The more you make me feel good, the happier I'll be and the* *better I'll look. Preach to me, Preacher. Tell me all about grace--, how I can do almost anything I want and get away with it. Don't wanna hear the law, that's old school. The happier I am, the better I'll look. And if I look good and feel good then surely the Bachelor will be attracted to **me**. I'll be a superstar, and everyone will love **me**."*

These attitudes make Grace-overloaded Bridezillas and Churchzillas. Where's the logic actually, when a man, the Bachelor **TELLS us** what He's looking for in a wife, but we insist on using the world's standards, or the standards of our own choosing to "adorn" ourselves? He doesn't want that. **If Jesus wanted the WORLD, He could have accepted Satan's first temptation** in the wilderness after He was Baptized by John the Baptist. *Just saying.*

Everybody wants to be a star, even some churches and their prideful leaders. The term, *Acquired Situational Narcissism,* (ASN) was coined by Robert B. Millman, Psychiatry professor at Cornell University's Weill Medical College. The Church is proud of Her pastor because he has letters and degrees from famous seminaries and divinity schools. They're proud because he knows all kinds of famous people. They're proud because he gets invitations to preach all over the world. He also has other churches coming to hear him preach at his own home church. How proud She is to host an event. Surely the outsiders must see how good this congregation has it. Surely this must be enviable; *"Our pastor is a star."*

Acquired Situational Narcissism differs from conventional narcissism in that it develops after childhood and is triggered and supported by our celebrity-obsessed society. I notice more and more at "church" events that people who come to hear the guest preacher, are taking pictures of, and selfies WITH him **<u>during</u>** the preaching event to prove that they were there. At any preaching event, the Word of God is a star, the anointing is the star, not the messenger. Media might play into the idea that this local congregation or pastor might be more important than other churches or pastors. Some ministries or their pastors are often on the news or in the pages of newspapers, or magazines. This could spawn a narcissism problem that might have been only a tendency or latent possibility, while media is helping it to become full blown *Narcissism Personality Disorder*.

In its presentation and symptoms, *Acquired Situational Narcissism* is indistinguishable from *Narcissistic Personality Disorder*, except its latent onset and it is supported a lot of others. The *Acquired Situational Narcissism* sufferer has unstable relationships, substance abuse, and erratic behavior.

Ironically, as his reputation grew, Dr Millman, himself developed *Acquired Situational Narcissism* and suffered from many of its symptoms. Dr Millman, from what I learned, did not profess Christ. He did not have the Word of God to guide him through his 15 minutes of fame. He had the heavy Brick of Grace and no Brick of Truth. *Acquired Situational Narcissism* could be a disorder relegated only to the unsaved, the unbelieving, the unconverted. What did I just say here? Yes, I said what I said, there's no excuse for a pastor who not only confesses Christ but also *represents* Christ to behave this way. There's no winking at the church who has let what God has given Her go to Her head, and God will deal with the **head** of that local congregation first.

Some of us have seen the television show *Bridezilla*. We see the bride's mood swings, her histrionics, her tantrums, her evil. We see the poor guy, the groom just standing there and marrying her anyway. Christ won't do that. **Christ will not marry Her, *anyway***. He will not marry her IN *any* way. This is proved out in the Book of the Revelation where John the Divine outlines the shortcomings of each of the Seven Churches, as was shown and told to him in prophetic visions. For example, the first Church was not acceptable as She was, because She had left her first love. Most who leave their first love wander about and then choose a new love, and that is usually another *person*, but Bridezilla most often leaves a first love to fall in love with herself, or she leaves because she is already in love with herself.

I am not saying that the entire Body of Christ, the entire Church today tends to be full of Herself. Not all churches; please not by any means. I have seen and been in some phenomenal Houses where the leadership is exceptional and godly. But I've also been in some so-called churches that grieve my Spirit and break my heart. I've seen churches in love with themselves, and to me for no apparent reason; there's been next to nothing in those churches to love.

The Narcissistic Church has unstable relationships. She has unstable relationships with other churches. She has unstable relationships with the community in which she sits. She looks like her pastor because it all flows from the head. There are many unstable relationships within the members as well. Divorce in the Church is approaching 52%. Recent studies show cliques run rampant in the Narcissistic Church. There's little to no brotherly love. The members of the various cliques believe and *say* that they love each other, but they usually don't love anybody else--, neither members nor strangers. This is usually evidenced by the members saying, *"We like a small church; we want to stay small."* To me, this means Church is a club and they want to control how many members can "join." What if Jesus had said, **We want a small Heaven?** No, He says, that God does not want one to be lost. Not one.

Collectively, that small-minded, narcissistic, me-minded church may not have won two souls to the Lord in the past two years. They've even stopped giving *altar calls* because no one comes up. It's dying, actually, but they haven't yet acknowledged that. They desperately need repentance, which leads to revival.

The Narcissistic Church has erratic behavior. You don't know if She's coming or going. When a family doesn't get along, it is the blame of the father, the inappropriate father, the distant father, the absent father, the uncaring father, the abusive father, and the weak father. The father's input, or lack thereof, creates unstable, dysfunctional families. Parents must teach and train their children to like work, because trouble is the usual outgrowth of excessive idleness. The same is true of the local assembly. Clique churches are usually well off, idle, and ridden with identity crises, gossip, insecurity, and other sins, as well as being purposeless.

The Narcissistic Church has problems with substance abuse as the members try to self-medicate their emotional pain. This is no mystery; even church people use everything from recreational substances to prescription drugs and freely purchase alcohol to abuse. **Faith, on the other hand, is also a substance**. It is the substance of things hoped for and in the Narcissistic Church, faith is abused to believe for things that have nothing to do with church, but instead the trappings of the world. The Narcissistic Church, being self-centered and in pain also abuses the members in that congregation. Hurting people, hurt people.

You may ask. Why doesn't She seek deliverance for this hurt and pain? Are you kidding? Deliverance is not pretty. Deliverance is messy. Plus, a narcissist doesn't believe that there's anything wrong with him, or her. They've *arrived* in life, so why would they seek deliverance?

I warn that only those who are **called** of the Lord should try to touch, teach, lead, or instruct God's anointed, called-*out* ones. Teachers will be judged more harshly than those who do not profess to be teachers. The blood of those whom you instruct will either be on your hands or the corresponding jewels for success will be in your crown.

Sin presents another whole issue. If the virgins in the parable did not commit sexual sins or Sins of Covenant, then they were still virgins-- *technically*. **Unbelief is sin. Laziness is sin. Ignorance is sin.** Not moving in purpose-- **Disobedience is sin. Stubbornness is sin.** Yes, regarding the virgins, if they didn't trim their lamps, they sinned. So, they could have sinned and still maintained their *sexual* virginity; but they were *no longer virgins to sin*. They could still be virgins, but still not be accepted. Illegal, unsanctioned sex is not the only sin.

...and I John saw the holy City, New Jerusalem coming down from God out of heaven, prepared as a bride adorned for her husband. (Revelations 21:2)

Without Spot, Blemish, or Wrinkle

The Holy City is prepared and adorned for her husband. A church is a community; it is a city; it is described as a House. In a House, the Lord puts everything that the House, community, or city would ever need. Forays into the world are only for evangelism purposes, they are not for entertainment purposes. Excursions into the world are dangerous, as the world is enticing. The world is destructive. The world destroys, it doesn't give life. The world destroys everything that it is allowed to own or control. Seduction into worldliness creates deep defects in that which is perfect, which goes against what the Church is called to be.

Without spot, blemish, wrinkle or any such thing is the criteria for the Bride of Christ. Narcissism is a spot, a blemish, *and* a wrinkle. Recall that Acquired Situational Narcissism begins when one is a little older and feels as though he or she has *arrived*. Having relationship with the world, that is loving the world is sin. Christ's Bride must be a virgin. Virgins have not had an intimate relationship with anyone or anything, including the world; She is waiting for her groomsman--, only.

She has not sold out to the world. She may not have ever experienced the world, ideally. She knows little to nothing about the world other than how to traverse it, to pluck sinners from the fire that the enemy set eons ago to consume them. The Church shouldn't look anything like the world; She is in it, but not *of* it. She doesn't wear the world's clothes. She doesn't adorn herself in their hairstyles, makeup, or perfumes. She is holy and set apart. Every trip into the world is to snatch a perishing soul, not to entertain Her own flesh and soul.

She has not known prostitution and has not been pimped in a natural or spiritual sense. She has not prostituted herself for money, goods, or gifts of any kind, especially to maintain her virginity. She has not let any of the world into her in any way, not sexually, not mentally, not physically, not intellectually. She does not think as the world thinks and does not think *on* things on which the world thinks.

The Church must be congruent in Spirit and in Truth. She cannot be Spirit only, super-fake holy, or mystical. She cannot be Truth only spouting off fire and brimstone Scriptures as punishments for broken or unfulfilled Law that none of us can keep anyway. There must be balance. She must know the Word, do the Truth, and also walk by the Spirit so that She does not fulfill the lust of the flesh.

And according to the Bible, She is to make herself <u>ready</u>. The leader of the flock has the responsibility to help, instruct, lead, and direct the Church's readiness for the Lamb. I lament that in today's churches we need to pray earnestly for good shepherds who have the right skill sets to lead the various congregations that will merge into the Church that Christ will be pleased with, and will unite with Him, prophetically.

Solomon's House took the Queen of Sheba's breath away. The order, the uniforms, and the service was amazing to her. Solomon's House was all together. Well, that was how it appeared to Sheba, remember Sheba wasn't saved. The Church will be scrutinized even more closely than that at the Lord's coming. Of course, the Lord sees the big picture of all the churches collectively and regionally, but few have taken my breath away. The Women that symbolize the Church need help. God-given pastors, good expository preaching and teaching, right spiritual impartation, faithful obedience, and diligence to the Word and to leadership will take away those spots, stains, blemishes, and wrinkles.

Whoso findeth a wife findeth a good thing and obtain the favor of the Lord, (Proverbs 18:22)

The Seven Women

I do not think that is easy to raise children. I have not given birth to any, but I have had both the joy and heartache of raising three children of relatives at different times in my life. One was a teenager when I got her. I only raised her for about a school semester so she could finish high school and accept her full scholarship to college. The other was a grade schooler who was only with me a short time. The third was a newborn and I raised her to nearly three years old. And then she lived with me again in kindergarten. All were girls.

Many say that raising girls is far more difficult than raising boys. Some say for the obvious reason that you have to protect the girls from the boys when they become teenagers. Others say that girls are too prissy and require too much time, attention, and spend too much money at the mall. I don't know if either or both of these things are true.

If I had given birth, I believe that I would have had a different perspective and grace for child rearing than I do. I hope so. For this reason, I say that I have not yet been *called* to raise children only asked, and usually by my mother, whom I chose to honor, so it would be well with me in the Earth.

In summary, I tried my hand at the rearing of three females for a short time to get them through various life situations.

The Church and hence, the "Women" of the Revelation are seven. Coincidentally, my father and mother gave birth to seven daughters. Even though we are different, we have many similarities. You can tell, for instance, by hearing any of our voices that we are in the same family. We may not all look alike, but when you see us together, you can tell that we belong together. If the Lord were to line all seven of us up, He might not be able to give commendations to our parents for any of us at this time. We are still works in progress. Thank God for Grace and time to get it right with the Lord.

What I'm saying is that I believe that my parents were *called* to raise the children that were born to them, and it's not an easy thing. If it were, we would all be perfect and ready for the Lamb, right now. How difficult it must be to rear children and/or churches if one is **not** *called* to do that? Which may be the reason why churches today look as they do. How difficult it must be to prepare a church when you *are called* to it evidenced by the judgments pronounced in the Book of the Revelation, how impossible and desperate one must be when one is **not <u>called</u>** to it.

We met the Bachelor, and we know what He's about. Now let's meet the Seven Women who are in line for His hand.

Seven being the perfect number. It could be possible as John looks at the Seven Churches of Asia Minor, which was ancient Mysia and is modern day Turkey. Seven represents fullness and wholeness, and it should represent perfection. I believe by choosing seven, the Lord's expectation is that these churches would have reached *perfection*, (maturity), by the time of their evaluations.

The Churches of Asia Minor were planted and parented, as it were, by the Apostles, who were called, appointed, and anointed men of God who were not just told to plant churches but were also <u>graced</u> to do it. Their Mommas didn't tell them to do it; God did, and God gave them special anointing to accomplish their tasks. God knows that I may or may not have been anointed to raise those three little girls, but I believe that God did give me some *grace* for it. But I also believe that He mostly gave the grace to rear those children to their birth parents, with whom they should have been residing.

Ephesus

Ephesus is the first of seven women, the first Church addressed in Chapter Two of the Book of the Revelation. This Church was planted by Paul, ministered to by John, and shepherded over by Timothy, a young man of excellent character and spirit, although raised spiritually by his grandmother and perhaps a single mother, as his father was not a believer. With a heritage and ministry like that, this Church should not have been slack in anything. In today's terms with the Bishop or Apostle like that and ministry guests such as prophets that come to that church, there should have been nothing missing, and nothing broken in Ephesus.

But there was.

Full of Grace and Truth, the Lord speaks to this Church. See the balance here. First, He gives acknowledgement of good works and diligence. The Church is not only being observed for good works, She also had to give account for idleness. Every man must give account and collectively every church as well.

Ephesus was a long-suffering Church. She did not complain; She did not faint in well doing. Ephesus could spot a broken vessel, a false prophet, a false apostle, and discreetly deal with them. She hated sin and was not slack about dealing with it. Of note, Ephesus is the only of the Seven Churches to whom

Paul wrote an epistle that is published in our Bible. Smyrna, Pergamum, Sardis, Philadelphia, Thyatira, and Laodicea have no published letters to them in the New Testament. Paul also wrote a letter to the Romans and to Churches in Greece.

God is Jealous, and Ephesus had become lax in Her passion for the Lord. It is stated that She had lost Her first love. Also, of note here is that Ephesus is the city where the Pagan *goddess*, Diana is worshipped. Idolatry, being the dominant culture, some of the Church may have fallen back into their old patterns. When one first falls in love the object of that Love is ***all*** she wants to think about and talk about. But when quality and quantity of time is not spent with the object of affection, the lover may become slack, and the love may wane.

Jesus' rebuke to this Woman, the Church of Ephesus is, **"Remember where you fell, repent and do again the first works, or else the Lord says that He will remove the candle stick from that place."** The candlestick represents the presence of the Lord. In the vernacular, *"If you don't pay any attention to me, I will leave you."*

As a woman, is Ephesus taking the groom for granted? He needs to feel love as well as first loving Her. This had become a one-sided love affair and that is not acceptable to the Lamb. She was not high maintenance, but this first potential Bride was beautiful when she was first born, when She was young, but a diversion happened instead of a conversion. That diversion was that She left Her first love.

The Bachelor may be asking Her, *"Where is the love?"*

Thank God for Grace and Mercy. Even though the Lamb states what is wrong with this Church now, He tells Her what to do to correct the matter and how to enter in victoriously. ***To him that overcometh will I give to eat of the tree of life which is in the midst of the paradise of God.*** **Thank God for Grace and Mercy.**

Ephesus is modern day Ephesus or *Efes*, in Turkey.

Smyrna

The next letter is written to the Angel of the Church of Smyrna. The letter is about the Church, and it is addressed to the authority, who is the pastor of that Church. The authority in Heaven, God is speaking to the authority in the Earth over this proposed Bride, the pastor, who is over that particular Church.

John writes what he has seen and heard to the Church at Smyrna, which, was in a wealthy trade city. *Thou art rich.* To an average Joe, a rich bride may be enough to seal the deal right there. But not with the

Lord, because all the riches in Earth are nothing compared to the riches in Heaven. Jesus is richer than anyone's Earth-riches. He owns all the silver and the gold, and all the cattle on 1000 hills belong to Him. The Earth is the Lord's and the fullness thereof.

Jesus first offers comfort to Smyrna when He says He knows their poverty and their tribulations.

But there is a judgment, **"I know the blasphemy of them which say they are Jews and are not but are the synagogue of Satan."** He acknowledges that there are folks in church, but church *ain't* in them. Preachers don't preach sin like they used to. Oh, wait a minute, *used to when?* Preachers must not have preached sin 2000 years ago either, else Smyrna would not have received this bad report from the Lord. Today's preachers don't want to offend the "tithes and offerings." They preach *to* the money, not **against** the sin. If you offend a parishioner, usually the first thing they'll do is stop tithing or giving offerings and preachers know that.

I'm a dentist. At work I'm careful not to talk to the patient's wallet or insurance company, or the need. Rather, I talk to the person. In my profession, there are rules, and regulations against this, and it is unethical. A higher "board" governs me, but I also submit wholly to the Board that has licensed me in the State of Virginia. God, who is no respective persons, expects the Church and pastors especially, to have superior business ethics,

Christian morals and properly represent the Truth of His Word.

More judgment is spoken, **"He knows about the blasphemy of those who say they are Jews but are not."** This tribulation is not unto death, but what doesn't kill will strengthen the Church.

As a woman, Smyrna was persecuted to death. The name, *Smyrna* is related to death; it was an aromatic embalming substance used in Bible times. Smyrna might be the woman who would silently endure abuse and never do anything about it, hoping that *he* would change. The world didn't recognize these Christian churches, they were only noticed to mock, ridicule, or persecute. Smyrna didn't respond well to negative treatment; she may have retreated as a wallflower. She was a poor church and didn't or couldn't fight back. Like a poor, abused woman who couldn't leave the abuser because she had no means and no way out. Instead of feeling Her Help coming on, she succumbed.

The Bachelor may have been asking, *"Why didn't you fight for Me? Why didn't you fight for what you believed in? Why didn't you call on Me to help you win the battles?"*

Thank God for Grace and Mercy. For those that overcome the tribulation and are faithful unto death will receive a crown of life. The overcomers will not be hurt in the second death, they shall be resurrected after the first death because it is appointed unto every man once to die, then the second death will not harm them.

Modern day Izmir is the ancient city of Smyrna, it is called the "Pearl of the Aegean."

Pergamos

Pergamos is the third bride-wannabe. Pergamos carries in its etymology, the idea of a *tower* and also of *marriage*. This Church was in a hellish place. It is described as *where the seat of Satan is*. Historians suggest that it might have been the place where there was a temple to Zeus--, talk about the valley of the shadow of death. Talk about table set for the people of God, even in the presence of their enemies. Enemies were all around and probably always around. The people in this Body did not have renewed minds. They infected the minds and manners of the congregants and probably spouted unbelief.

There's a mention of faithful Antipas having been martyred and killed there sometime before 100 AD. He is said to have been one of Our Savior's first Disciples and a Bishop of Pergamon. And to have been put to death in a tumult whereby the priest of Aesculapius, the Greek *god* of medicine, who had celebrated health center in the temple in that city. *Oh thou that killeth the prophets...*

This Woman is told, *"**But I have a few things against thee, because thou hast there them that hold the doctrine of Balaam, who taught Balac to cast a stumblingblock before the children of Israel, to eat things sacrificed unto idols, and to commit fornication.**"* When Balak would not curse Israel, a devious plot was engineered to trip up the people of God. They were enticed with strange women, and many fell into sin. This so angered the Lord that He killed many of them. In that city, in that Church, among them were those who had participated in this plot against the Israelites, which caused the Lord to be angry against Israel, and He killed many of them.

Furthermore, this wanna-be-Bride was told, *"**So hast thou also them that hold the doctrine of the Nicolaitanes, which thing I hate.**"* The Nicolaitanes, which the Lord states here that He hates, themselves, were a sect of haters. They were prayer haters. Hating Christians, they performed hateful deeds and promoted a hateful doctrine. They were slack on Truth, filled with error, and mostly did their stuff hidden away as a secret society. Therefore, the Lord promised that He would come against them with the Sword of the Spirit or the Word of God. Verse 16 charges to ***repent quickly or He will come and fight with the Sword of his mouth***. Truthfully, since we do not live by bread alone, but by every Word that proceeds out of God's mouth, I would rather have His Living Word than a warring Word.

Despite all this, the Lord commands them that they **hold fast to His Name and to remain faithful, not denying Him.** However, He can't marry Pergamos because of certain issues, such as the doctrine of the Nicolaitanes, and certain ones that observe the doctrine of Balaam. There were some who taught that it was lawful to eat things sacrificed to idols, which represents a stumbling block for the young and those who do not know better. Some taught that fornication was no sin. Their worship was impure, and it drew men into impure practices, as Balaam did the Israelites.

As a woman, Pergamos is as a murmuring, complaining, whining bride, which makes her unattractive to a man. Further, she's uncaring, uncompassionate and dangerous to others, casting stumbling blocks before them.

The Bachelor might be saying to her, **"Pergamos I can't marry you because you don't love the things that I love and hate the things that I hate. We really don't have that much in common."**

Thank God for Grace and Mercy. There is a reward for repentance and overcoming. *"They shall eat of the hidden manna and have the new name and the white stone, which no man, knows except he that receiveth it."*

Pergamos is modern day Bergama, in Turkey.

So far, three out of three Churches are out of the running for marriage to the Lamb. As in *The Bachelor* show, He has not given any of them a rose and unless they repent, they must leave the show.

Thyatira

Enter the next contestant, Thyatira. Again. The letter is to the Angel of the house. This is a weighty matter, as if God is saying, **"Sir, this is why I cannot marry your daughter."** This would be like telling Moses, "Your people can't go in." The pastor is synonymous with Moses and the people who need to *go in* in Moses Day were the Israelites who came out of Egypt, and in our day, they are the people, the congregations who have come out of the wilderness of sin--, those who make up the Church.

Moses made a deal with God, saying that he would not go *in*, but asked God to let the people go in. Jesus has already done that, so anyone who doesn't go in this time, well the Scriptures say, *Let him who is blessed be blessed and he was damned be damned.*

This Church had some great qualities which are mentioned to her: faith, charity, service, patience, and fruitfulness. In this Church, however, there were wicked seducers who used the Name of God to lead the people into fornication and to eat things which were dedicated to idols. They were in direct competition with true ministers of God. These seducers were likened unto Jezebel, which is a spirit that is not specific to women. Where there's *Jezebel*, there's always an *Ahab spirit*. Both these *spirits* can be present in the **same** person--, hence your Dr. Jekyll and Mr. Hyde. Hence your bipolar types. Hence your demonically possessed types, male or female.

This Woman, who also had plans and hopes to marry the Bachelor, was evaluated and her sins were addressed. ***"Notwithstanding, I have a few things against thee because thou sufferest that woman Jezebel, which calleth herself a prophetess, to teach and to seduce my servants, to commit fornication, and to eat things sacrificed unto idols."***

Thyatira lacked zeal for the maintenance of godly discipline and doctrine, and indulged in error, so much so that falsehood and idolatry permeated, overlaid, and modified the whole character of the Church, obscuring the faith, deceiving the saints, and setting up in its very midst the school of Satan.

The first Christian in Thyatira was a woman. Looking at the origin of the name, Thyatira, *thygatira*, a daughter and a *thugateer*. We get the idea of feminine oppression. I suppose you are shocked as I am, but some of these first *thugs* were women. The false prophets who first enticed the women, the members of this church into apostasy, were **women** and that's thuggish behavior.

As a woman, I see the Church of Thyatira as a strong woman who overstepped Her authority and went too far. She went so far that She went into error and probably legalism and oppression. She might be the overbearing woman, probably very beautiful and seriously prone to narcissism. **Bridezilla-ism** and **Churchzilla-ism**. She might be attractive in the natural as Ing says that Jezebel is, but she would not be attractive spiritually, and most of all, not attractive to the Lamb of God. According to Apostle Dr. John Eckhardt, *"The Apostolic anointing releases the discernment the Church needs to resist infiltration of the enemy."* He further states, *"False doctrine and false teachers carry a **spirit of witchcraft**. There is no other explanation as to why people come under the control of false teaching that is contrary to the Scriptures."*

The Bachelor may have to tell her, **"You're not the boss of me."**

Pastors today are allowing idolatry in the House. Of course, parishioners are told to let the wheat and the tare grow together, and the Lord will separate them in the judgment. In other words, they're saying they aren't going to do anything about it. My Bible says that one sinner destroys a lot of good.

Most people think that idols are physical. A common idol is sex. I know too many who are fornicating regularly but still go to church. Just read some of the vanity license plates in your church parking lot and you can tell what's on the car owners' minds. Perhaps there's a member of the congregation who is self-gratifying and whose entire imagination revolves around sex—he/she is a sex addict. They are abundant in society **and** in local congregations. His mind is not renewed. He either hasn't been taught the Word and it hasn't been modeled before him. And or, deliverance hasn't been administered to him or her.

The Word of God will always be proved with signs and wonders such as deliverance. Does any deliverance happen in the church you attend? Or are the tares just growing alongside the wheat until Jesus comes?

It could be that someone you work with, someone who is not divorced from their husband, is shacked up with a man who's not divorced from his wife. But you hear them trying to teach others about Jesus. *What* Jesus would that be? The Jesus of their understanding, the Jesus that lets them do whatever seems good in their own eyes because they've been taught nothing, or they've been taught Grace with no Truth.

Christ is not thinking about marrying Thyatira as She is. Instead, He proclaims the judgment that will befall those who do not change and repent. He's going to throw Her and Her followers who won't repent into a bed of tribulation. The NIV translation says, *into a bed of pain*. Her children will be killed with death. That is the second death, leaving them with shame and everlasting contempt. Thank God for Grace and Mercy, for the Lord prophetically sees the value in this beautiful Woman. *And he that overcometh and keepeth my works till the end, to him will I give power over the nations, and he shall rule them with a rod of iron; as the vessels of a potter, shall they be broken to shivers; even as I received of my Father. And I will give him the morning star.*

Thyatira is the modern day Akhisar, noted today for its rugs. Lydia (Acts 16:14) traded here, and it was known for its purple dye.

Sardis

The next Woman in the lineup to hook up with the Bachelor is Sardis. Her name maybe derived from the Sardis stone, which was worn as an amulet to drive away fear or to encourage cheerfulness. Ebrard finds an etymological derivation denoting something *new* or *renewed.* And there is a further explanation which is derived it from a word that denotes a *builder's rule* or *measuring line.* Sadly, there's no Church of any kind in Sardis at this time. Sardis did not make it as a church or a city. Today it is only an archaeological digging site.

The Righteous Judge pronounced this over Sardis, *"Thou hast a few names, even in Sardis, which*

have not defiled their garments, and they shall walk with me in white, for they are worthy. I know thy works, that thou hast a name, that thou livest and art dead.

We are told in the New Testament to beware of the leaven of the Pharisees, which is hypocrisy. Decaying religion, along with hypocrisy, are the crimes laid on Sardis. Previously, She had flourished and had been good and honorable with a good reputation, but not so much anymore. Their doctrine had been pure, they had unity and no division in the house, excellence in worship; things were done decently and in order.

Well, it looked good on the outside.

They had a name that said, they lived, but they were dead. They had a *form* of godliness but denied the power thereof. They had taken a *name* to say we have a ***god*** and we have a religion, but they didn't really walk in it. They were living in image-driven life. They were religious and probably had every *i* dotted and every *t* crossed. Everything was surely by the book and not by the Spirit, much like the Pharisees. They were dead because the letter of the Law kills, and the Spirit gives life. They probably had dead services, dead souls, dead spirits, dead ministers, long monotonous prayers that probably hit the ceiling of the church, and crashed back down at their feet--, prayers that never left the room.

As a Woman, this Church was meticulous but boring. If She were filling out a dating questionnaire, She would have to indicate that She is **religious** but not *spiritual*. She probably looked really good on the outside, but there was no verve in her. There was no life. She probably wasn't interesting, much like many churches today, where all the teenagers leave as soon as they finish high school or become independent of their parents. Boring. Her House was probably perfect, but you couldn't touch anything.

The Bachelor might not ask Her anything; He'd probably be yawning.

Sardis could not maintain a foothold for Christianity in that area. As a matter of fact, all the seven of the Churches could not. Today 99% of Turkey is Muslim. Turkey is a secular country with freedom of religion, but the Islamic foothold was maintained for the 600 years prior to 1920, by the Ottomans. The Turks changed all of that in the 1920s, but Orthodox and Gregorian churches, Catholics, Suryanis, Protestant Christians, and Jews comprise the remaining 1% of those who practice their religion. Turkey is the only country among the Islamic countries which has included secularism in Her constitution and practices it.

Thank God for Grace and Mercy. Thank God for the Blood of Jesus. The reward of repentance and overcoming for Sardis is the promise of white raiment. Holiness has its own reward, and holiness is more than righteousness. But doing what is right, holiness is not doing what is common, but doing what is to be done, being what you should be when no one is looking. Christ imparts His righteousness to us, but holiness is something that we must put on ourselves. It is a choice, and when made and kept, He says He will not blot your name out of the Book of Life but will confess your name before the Father and before His angels.

Philadelphia

The Church of Philadelphia, the City of Brotherly Love--, there was no fault found with this Church. Humans, of course, are not perfect, but they had love, and love covers a multitude of sin. ***Because thou hast kept the word of my patience. I also will keep thee from the hour of temptation, which shall come upon all the world to try them that dwell upon the earth. Behold, I come quickly, hold that fast which thou hast that no man take thy crown.***

The Lord opens great and effectual doors of opportunity and ministry. He closes doors for the sinful and He closes doors when their season of being open is over. He shuts the door of Heaven against the foolish virgins who have slept away their day of Grace. The Church is as a precious virgin who should be making ready, trimming Her lamps, and preparing Herself for marriage to the Lamb. This Church is to undergo a time of *trial*, **not tribulation**.

As a woman, this Church had love for all and knew how to show it. She was probably prone to hospitality and preferred others to Herself. She probably knew how to forbear all things, endure all things, and hope all things. She is probably easy to get along with and had lots of friends.

The **Bachelor** may have asked Her, ***How you doin'?***

Thank God for Grace and Mercy. Thank God for the Blood of Jesus. By repentance and change, the overcomer shall be a stately pillar of honor in the Temple of God, upon which is written in honorable inscription. Being a pillar is substantial because Jesus is the Chief Cornerstone and also the Capstone. That puts you in good company, with the Lord as your foundation and head. The Lord is your beginning and your end your Alpha and your Omega, and you are an intimate relationship and purpose with the Lord. Amen.

Ancient Philadelphia is modern day Alasehir, Turkey.

Laodicea

Laodicea was lukewarm and without passion. This potential bride's name suggests ***mob rule*** being derived from, **laos**, meaning people and **dike**, meaning **judgment** or **justice**. This Church practiced, democracy, rather than theocracy. They decided things by popular opinion and voting creating a self-righteous, self-sufficient independent Church.

Thou *aren't neither cold nor hot, but worse than either. I would thou wert cold or hot. I will spew thee out of my mouth. Thou sayest, I am rich and increased with goods and have need of nothing And knowest not that thou art wretched and miserable and poor and blind and naked. I counsel thee to buy of me gold, tried in the fire that thou mayest be rich and white raiment, that thou mayest be clothed, and that the shame of thy nakedness do not appear, and anoint thine eyes with eyesalve that thou mayest see.*

This letter is about the *comme si, comme sa, que sera, sera* crowd. *I know thy works I would thou wert cold or hot. So then because thou art lukewarm, and neither cold nor hot, I will spue thee out of my mouth.* A lukewarm people (Church) does not rightly divide the Word. They don't necessarily *hear* error, false teaching, or false prophets. Neither do they defend the truth. They do not have spiritual ears. As Christians, we have a charge to be able to give an answer for what we believe. We are charged to discern, *trying every spirit*. I believe the basis for this pathetic lack of passion is that the Laodiceans do not *know* the Word of God.

They may be just going through the motions of religion, and no conversion has been made in their heart.

The Lord is exhorting Laodicea to get off the fence and go one way or the other. Laodicea is a noncommittal Church.

As the **Bachelor**, you wouldn't know if this Woman was *into* you or not. She would show you no passion.

I dated a fellow like this once; he called me at 10:30 every night to say goodnight. We talked for about four or five minutes. And that was what he thought constituted a relationship. He didn't call me or talk to me any other time during the day, but he would arrive at my house like clockwork Friday and Saturday evening to spend time together. If he hadn't have called at all, I could have called him cold. Had he called in the morning to say top of the morning to you, or bless the Lord, it's a new day and taken me to lunch now and again, and talked with passion about our budding relationship, I could have called him hot. But he was neither hot nor cold. He was lukewarm, and it was confusing to me.

This fellow obviously didn't know me because I have a hot or cold effect on people. They love me or they hate me, but almost nobody who knows me is lukewarm to me.

Now, I don't believe that lukewarmness can confuse the Lord, either because God is one of those all or nothing kind of guys Himself--, and He knows it. You love Him or you don't. And you don't need to pluck the petals out of a daisy to know which one. God cannot be fooled by the lukewarm. A man, a woman, a church that behaves this way, has an identity problem. She also has a purpose and a passion problem. She doesn't know who She is, or what She wants. Many people play this game in the natural, hedging their bets because they don't know who will be in power tomorrow? But As for today, they don't want to rock the boat.

Laodicea thought she *had it going on* and that she didn't need anything. Jesus knew, but She didn't know that She was wretched, and miserable, and poor, and blind, and naked. Most people cannot see themselves as they go through their foolishness and drama. It is not until someone confronts them with Truth or shows them a tape of themselves that they even realize how petty or evil they may have been.

This Bridezilla is not even properly dressed. Naked is embarrassing, but in that culture to have on the wrong garment was devastating. There She was, naked and blind, and not in a Statue of Lady Justice kind of way but standing there like a pitiful waif or orphan who doesn't even know that she is not dressed properly for *marriage*. I've always been taught to wear your best before royalty. Bible tells me that. **Kings' daughters were among your honorable women at your right hand stands the queen in gold from Ophir. The royal daughter is all glorious within the palace; Her clothing is woven with gold. She shall be brought to the King and robes of many colors; The virgins, her companions who follow her, shall be brought to you with gladness and rejoicing they shall be brought. They shall enter the King's palace.**

What must this Pastor have either been doing or going through trying to get this Church prepared for the Lamb!

I note here that in the Old Testament they prepared the Lamb for the people, as in the Passover. But in the New Testament the **people** must be prepared for the Lamb! Hallelujah!

Yet Christ, in His long-suffering, patiently stands at the door and knocks on the hearts of the unbelievers and spiritual offenders. He patiently waits, but He will not always strive with man. Harden, not your heart, and answer in the day provocation; answer the door, answer the Lord.

As a Woman, I think this Church, Laodicea could be talked into anything. She didn't really have a backbone, no strong belief system. She might not have known *what* She believed. She may have been considered two-faced, agreeing with whomever was talking at the time.

The **Bachelor** may have said to her, as I did to the lukewarm suitor, *"You're just not that into me."*

Thank God for Grace and Mercy. Thank God for the Blood of Jesus. This apathetic *Que Sera, Sera* Church acting on their own choices, independent of the Lord might come to repentance and still be an overcoming Church. There's much Wisdom in Godly counsel. If they could hear what the Spirit is saying and make repentance and amends, they could still *enter in* and sit down with the Lord on His Throne. ***As I also overcame and have sat down with my father on his throne.***

As the Lord exemplifies Grace and Truth, we see that both are necessary and acknowledge, because six of the seven Churches have both good things and bad things about them.

Pastors, like all good men who have daughters are determined that their daughter will marry a good man. Will *his* daughter be a great bride for the good man? Most believe so. Most believe that the hardest part is to **find** a husband that's good enough for his little girl. Many narrow-sighted are looking for a man that's good enough for their not-so-good, probably spoiled daughter. Likewise, pastors have to be bishops, fathers, and overseers; they cannot lose sight of the fact that their church, the local congregation is to be prepared for the Lamb. The pastor doesn't have to search for a **man** for this Daughter of Zion, the Church, so he can spend more dedicated time preparing his **big girl**, the local assembly that he watches over, to make Her ready for the Lamb, Who is already ready.

They prepared the lamb for the people, as in the Passover, but in the New Testament the <u>people</u> must be prepared for the Lamb.

And in that day, I will turn the hearts of the fathers to the children and the hearts of the children back to the fathers. (Malachi 4)

And he shall go before him in the spirit and power of Elias, to turn the hearts of the fathers to the children and the disobedient to the wisdom of the just to make ready a people prepared for the Lord. (Luke 1:17)

The Crisis of False Shepherds

The Old Testament recounts time and again of false and corrupted shepherds. You can read it yourself in the major prophets such as Jeremiah, Ezekiel, and Isaiah. The origins of these false shepherds are manifold. The net result is that they are **not** fathers to the congregation, which desperately needs fathers in a society that is devastatingly fatherless. False shepherds simply are **not fathers**. Some of them have not been fathered themselves. These fatherless "fathers" include those who ran away from a church home to start their **own** churches whose ministries are not sanctioned.

Unfathered and or fatherless fathers also are created when boys are told by their husband-abandoned mothers, that they are the **man** of the house in their broken homes. These broken boys are thrust into leadership positions even in the church. There, they then create *what they are.* They create broken churches. Nobody is raising the kids, or the congregation. He's not the daddy or father of the House, just the **man**. *Man* is not a term of relationship. Father, husband, and son are. However, *Man* is the term of individualism, a term of aloneness.

Now that he's older, this guy who's been in charge at his mom's house since he was seven, who has always been used to being in charge, believes that he is the *man, but* in a bad way. **The Man** usually refers to the person or collective persons in charge. It refers to authority figures in general, such as the police. *The Man* is colloquially defined as the figurative person who controls our world. *The Man* is also often used to denote the boss of a workplace.

Churches led by fatherless and unfathered fathers do not acknowledge God as Father. They also have no clue as to *how* to father, so he usually just exerts his **manhood** on the church. His manhood is usually his sense of authority, position, and privilege. Flesh, and many times, toxic.

Sometimes in all of this exertion, the church becomes the false pastor's puppet, and *he* is actually the *Bridezilla* manipulating the world around him and exalting himself. How does he *look* sitting in his highchair? How shiny is his big ring? How does his voice sound over the state-of-the-art sound system?

How does he *look* when he preaches? How does he look when he shouts? How many fall on the floor when he prays? Flesh, flesh, flesh.

As it pertains to the Parable of the Ten Virgins, five had their lamps trimmed and five didn't. If the preacher is not leading imparting and teaching, there is no way the virgin lamps can be lit. That is Leading, Imparting, and Teaching—*LIT*. Leading, Imparting and Teaching will cause the lamps to be lit. If the preacher is in his flesh, then he can't take anyone into the Spirit. If the preacher is not trying to take the people into spiritual revelation, information, and impartation, then he may create any number of *kinds* of churches, such as the Clique Church, the Event Church, the Project Church, or the Church of That's-How-It's-Always-Been-Done: tradition.

The nature and responsibility of the Ministerial Office is not a lordship but a service. Ministers are to be servant leaders. This service is not commanded by man, but by God. It is the business of the Angel (pastor) to hear for the church, receive for the church and to answer for the church which has been committed to his care. He is the Watchmen of the flock. He has to present the Word that is gotten from God faithfully to His people, and to see that it is accepted, observed, and obeyed according to the true intent of its divine Author. To the Heavenly Angels God addresses His judgments, His rebukes and His directions, as if the whole estate of the Churches were wrapped up in them and they alone are responsible for that estate. In obeying his directives and answering his God-given call, he will raise up a flock of people prepared and made ready for the Lord.

Degrees of Separation

Six degrees of separation refers to the idea that if a person is one step away from each person he or she knows and two steps away from each person who is known by one of the people he or she knows, then everyone is an average of six steps away from each person on Earth.

Six is the number of man. So if a man is separated from God by six steps or degrees, then he really doesn't *know* God. He only knows man and what that man knows *about* God. He might know *of* God, but he doesn't **know** God. To have relationship, one must **know** the person for him or herself. The same is true with the Lord.

If I don't **know** a person, I cannot introduce him to anyone. If a man, for example, is the keynote speaker and I am the emcee at an event, I can *read* his introduction from a paper. I can announce him, but I can't really *introduce* him to anyone. I can speak of his education, his speaking experience, and the names of his family members, but I am not really *introducing* him because I can't tell you what I know about him from personal experience. Likewise, the pastor can read what he knows *of* God, what he got from parts of the Bible, a dictionary, another man's sermon, or books; but unless there's been personal, quality time spent with the Lord, that Preacher doesn't **know** God. If you don't know God and got your sermon out of a book or from a website, you will only introduce the man who wrote your sermon--, the man who gave you that saying or cliche, the man who told you what you are now repeating.

How many times have I heard in a church **as the sermon**, *"I was watching television this morning before church, and this is what Joel Osteen said?"* I already know what Joel Osteen said. I watched that show this morning too, as I was getting dressed for church.

What did **God** say? If there a Word from the Lord, or at least what did you *hear* from the LORD, when Joel Osteen said what he said? Did you go to the Bible after you heard this thing that seems so worthy of repeating? Was there revelation within you from God? What did God say about what Osteen said? Nothing? Anything?

You don't know Him, and He *ain't* talking to you. If you did, you'd tell me what God said because it is far more interesting, more exciting, revelatory and life changing than what Osteen said. Furthermore, as the pastor, it is your charge to convey what the **Lord** said to the congregation, not Osteen to your congregation and not Osteen *for* your congregation.

Can't introduce Him if you don't know Him.

Whole congregations are sitting on pews every Sunday and Wednesday listening to an entertainer who might know *things* about God but doesn't know God. Sadly, some don't know *things* about God, the "sermon" is a series of jokes, euphemisms, cliches. How wearisome.

If the introduction has never been made by the pastor to his congregation, then She (The Church) doesn't know Him, either.

No one has made the introduction so the Church may have 50% with trimmed lamps, and 50% without their lamps lit. I don't know. She might look good. There may be leaves on the fig tree, but where are the figs? Will She prepare *Herself* for the Groom, the Lamb of God? Will she bring an offering, suitable as Abel did instead of Cain? I ask because Abel had visitation and intimacy with the Lord. Cain came like the fig tree, with only vegetation.

If you ever meet Jesus, unless you are the most demonically possessed soul living, you will **love** Him. He is irresistible. If you ever meet Him and accept and experience His love for you, you will wanna be with Him, near Him, in Him forever. He's the lover of your soul, the greatest lover. The cares of this world may distract, but truthfully, if you spend any time with Him, you will love Him and crave Him. You will hunger and thirst after Him. You will chase Him. That is, if anyone ever makes the introduction to you.

If no one ever makes the introduction, there's no way you can love Him because you won't know Him.

For introducing the Lord, which a good preacher is to make every time he gets up to preach, might sound something like, *"I know, because I was there."* Or it may be, "*I know because He told me.*" Or "He showed me. I know because that's how I got from here, from where I was to where I am. I know because that's how I got out of that horrible situation. I know because that's how He saved me and blessed me." I heard Tommy Bates singing a song the Lord gave him. ***I Know Because It Happened To Me.***

Now that preacher can make an introduction. Not because of how well he can sing or write songs, but because of his life, his testimony, and his relationship with the Lord.

When a preacher doesn't talk about God as a person with whom he has relationship, when he doesn't speak of the Lord as an acquaintance, friend, or brother, or even as a lover of his soul, then he probably does not have a relationship with Him. If he has no relationship, he can never make an introduction. Chances are pretty good that if he doesn't know God whom *he* is pretending to represent. But he hasn't taken the time to know you either. Does the preacher of the small to moderate-sized church you've been attending for 20 years even know your name, or which of the small people in children's church belong to your family?

Great and Swelling Speeches

Great and swelling speeches is another name for random ramblings if you let me tell it. Of note, after every assessment of the Seven Churches of the Revelation, there is the phrase, ***He that hath an ear, let him hear what the Spirit sayeth unto the churches.*** Seven times this is repeated. When He says something once, it's important. When God says something twice, better listen! When God says something three times—woe! This may be the only time when God says the exact thing SEVEN TIMES! This is a severe warning! But how does a man hear? How can he hear? He only hears if the preacher has been sent and if the preacher is preaching. Preaching what? Preaching what thus saith the Lord, else the man is only introducing Joyce Meyer, TD Jakes, or Joel Osteen.

In order to properly grow a Christian and a Christian Church, they must be **fed** the Word of God. The Church has not majored in the things She should have. She has majored in the *minors*. The Church has focused on or been taught things of minor importance rather than things of major importance. But what was preached probably sounded good when it was preached. Folks probably shouted, *Amen!* Some may have jumped up, waved their hands, shouted, Hallelujah. The more agile or the more moved may have made a circuit or two around the sanctuary, but it may not have been more than a swelling speech with swell promises that didn't have much to do with the Word of God.

Plowing With God's Heifer

Then we have the preachers who are just doing a job. Once I asked the pastor of a church where I was a member a Bible question on a Sunday afternoon, after church. He chuckled and told me that he was, **"Off the clock."**

Just once. I didn't waste my time after that.

You have your hirelings.

Judges 14:18 refers to plowing with another man's heifer, which means to take advantage of that man. Too many preachers are trying to build a name for themselves by using the church as their Fortune 500 company to support their families in lavish style and pay their expenses to live in luxury. I know of one man who has named *his* church after himself. (I kid you not.)

The Hireling takes the wealth from the sheep, leaving them lacking or desolate. He does not look for those who are lost. He does not bind up the broken hearted. Neither will he carry the lame on his shoulders and minister to them. He does not visit the sick and shut-in or the locked up. He will not lay down his life for them; it is all about him.

Jesus said more than once. *If you love me, feed my sheep.* The Hireling will not, and often cannot feed the sheep. He "feeds" them the same old rambling fodder from weak to wake. I mean, week to week. They're milk fed at best, creating veal that go from weak to weaker and are easy prey for the enemy.

We Have Not Many Fathers

We have not many fathers. Personally, I have known so-called pastors who hate children, don't want any, didn't want any, can't stand the ones they have. They feel trapped in their marriages or have bounced from two to three, or even evicted a fourth wife out. Yet they believe that they represent a God who is all about covenant, who is all about family, who's all about marriage and relationship, and who suffers the little children to come unto Himself. That's the same as working for the athletic shoe company, but you hate athletic shoes wouldn't be caught dead in a pair, and you'll only wear dress shoes or loafers.

These kinds of pastors are not true fathers. Neither are they adoptive fathers. They aren't even foster parents or babysitters. They are spiritual defectives and defectors. They are double agents. They are hirelings who have been hired by an unsuspecting congregation or have appointed themselves to the position for the perks. God's people are paying them, but since they are not for God, they are against Him. Therefore, they work for Satan.

It is really difficult enough to be a leader, even if you're called to be one. It takes discipline, diligence, a *calling*, and a commensurate anointing for what you're called to do. But to pretend to be a leader must be discouraging and disheartening to both the perpetrator and the members. God gives both Grace and anointing to lead if that is what one has been called to do.

A hallmark of a leader is one who knows how to unify the parts to make a whole. In order to lead a local congregation, the leaders must unify them and lead, impart and teach to them individually and as a group. Cliques cannot be unified into the whole; they're elitist, who will not associate with "those people." Events are only distractions for the moment and usually do not unify the people for any length of time. Projects are only temporary goals that can't unify either. Tradition is usually religion and religion is not leaving the planet, nor are religious folks.

These unprepared "churches" are led by false, egotistical pastors who do not know how to set the Body in order because they are not *called* to do it and won't listen to the prophets and apostles who know. The Lord has promised in the Major Prophets that these pastors will utterly be cut off from the Earth.

A leader is one who knows the way goes the way and shows the way.
John Maxwell

Cherem, devoted or devoted thing; anything set aside for God's use.

Saying touch, not mine anointed, and do my prophets no harm. (1 Chronicles 16:22 and Psalm 105:15)

Touch Not Mine Anointed

Touch not mine anointed generally means in churches where I've sat, "Don't talk about the man of God." He usually hides behind this phrase when he has no intention of being accountable to God or the people of God. To a lesser degree, this phrase may mean, on a good day, "*Don't talk about the <u>woman</u> of God*," --, but she's just a woman--, so? God loves women and He is no respecter of persons. The Church is a Woman. She is God's Woman, and She is of greater importance to God than you may have ever realized. That anointed Woman is His Church.

Touch not God's Church.

She is anointed to *become* the Bride of Christ, just as the man is given authority to *become* a son of God. So, the Woman, this local congregation is to culminate into One to form the Church with the *anointing* to *become* the Bride of Christ. It is a process, and She is anointed to grow, mature, learn, prosper, to be and to do good works. **Becoming one.** She could channel all that anointing into a selfish endeavor, or she could use it to become glorious in the Earth, to the glory of God. Most of the time the choice of good or bad falls on the shoulders of the leader, who, if he is good, produces good fruit and good results such as a good Church. But if he's bad, the Church defaults and goes the way of the flesh, or the world, or begins to look just like him and his bad self. Good tree, good fruit; bad tree, bad fruit.

Well, who would want to *touch* God's Church? Any number of committed sinners who plan to stay that way. Any number who are living under the lies and falsehoods that the Church is not a viable entity with purpose and destiny. Any number of error laden idiots might want to touch, use, or abuse His anointed.

No man can enter into an intimate relationship with the Church or its members. She must remain a virgin. Even the shepherd or the shepherdess of the House has not known Her intimately. That is reserved for Christ.

You cannot have sex with Christ. When you fornicate with the members of the church. It's like having sex with Jesus.

When some tried to *know* the Church or approach knowing the Church intimately (OT temple prostitutes), literally the Sons of Belial, Phineas and Hophni were slain by the Lord. In the New Testament, it is made clear that Jesus will have no concord with Belial. Those who take the Church, (Her members) on as sex objects are Sons of Belial, be it any individual member or the entire Body.

Similarly, staining or soiling the Church that you shepherd defiles Her. The Bride Groom doesn't want a defiled bride. Pastor, why spend all those years all your life ministering to a church that will be rejected by God? The Seven Churches in Asia Minor are real examples of things that churches **cannot** grow to be if they are to be accepted by the Lamb.

Preacher, spoiling your church so they will *like you* because you let them do whatever they want, whenever they want, ignoring the Word of God and even His prophets that He sends before judgment in any House, or instead of judgment in His great Mercy toward us, is unwise. A spoiled child is no fun to be around, and adults and other children will usually shun him. It will be hard for him to find and keep a mate, so it will be with the church that you spoil, giving them *your* rules and letting them have *their* way all the time instead of feeding them God's laws and God's ways will not raise up a church that the Bridegroom could ever want, even if it's 50,000 members.

Using the church that you shepherd for your own personal gain is spiritual abuse, and God will deal with you as well as the church itself for allowing itself to be used in that way. That's plowing with God's heifer.

Figuratively, putting the church before your family will cause you to raise a very dysfunctional and or rebellious family and church--, whether or not you're the pastor. Having starving children in your home while you give generous offerings at church will not create children who understand or are tolerant of church. Paying your tithes is another thing completely. Spending every waking hour in the evenings and weekends to the exclusion of your family will not build your family. The family is the building block of that local church. Pastor or minister, or any leader you can't have a more intimate relationship with the church than you do with your own family. God did not call *you* to marry the church. God has a Groom for the Church, already.

If you're not the pastor of the church, you can't do that. If you are the pastor of the church, you really can't do that.

Further proof that you are *getting* what God is teaching in the church is walked out in your home life. Your home life should be better. Your spouse and children should be well adjusted, healthy, and happy. When the joy of Heaven comes into your home, then you know that you're doing what you're supposed to be doing regarding the church and church is doing what it is supposed to be doing for you. If what you're teaching the congregation doesn't manifest in the home, you may not be *getting it* at all.

For anyone who eats and drinks without discerning the body eats and drinks judgment upon himself? That is why many of you are weak and ill and some have died.
(1Corinthians 1)1:29-30, RESV

Not Discerning the Body

Not discerning the Body, many are sick and many die. If you were not to recognize a part of your own body, you wouldn't minister to it. You might not feed it. You might not clothe it. You might not take care of it if it were hurting or sick. In short, you would abuse it.

Not discerning the Lord's Body, many are sick, many sleep --, that is, many are dead. There are things that normally, in a non-teaching church, the congregants are **not** taught. Ephesians outlines the Fivefold Ministry gifts that the Lord has put in the Body to edify it. *and He Himself gave some to be apostles some prophets some evangelists and some pastors and teachers for the equipping of the saints for the work of ministry for the edifying of the body of Christ till we all come to the unity of faith and of the knowledge of the son of god to a perfect man to the measure of the stature of the fullness of Christ but speaking the truth in love may grow up in all things into him who is the head Christ from whom the whole body* *joint in it together by what every joint supplies according to the effective working by which every part does its share causes growth in the body for the edifying of itself in love.*

Being in a family, if you don't discern or are taught that someone is in your family, then you may not treat them as you treat family. The same applies for people in the church who are also considered family. The same applies to the entire Church, which is and has a particular relationship to Christ that is over and above the natural relationship that the entire Church has to any person, notwithstanding the individual relationships within that body.

The farmer takes a wife; the preacher already has one. Books have been written and messages preached about pastors who take their local congregation on as their "mistress." Some have said that the pastor's wife simply has to understand and forebear. That creates two problems, the first being that the preacher/pastor already has wife, and he is in a spiritual covenant with her, and he has promised not to forsake her in his wedding vows. So how can he take on a *mistress*, even if it is the church? That's spiritual adultery. To me, that's almost the same as robbing a bank for a good reason, such as Grandma needed surgery.

That local church and the Church collectively already has a man, His name is Jesus. Well, it's supposed to be if She is focused and prepares for marriage to the Lamb. It should be built into this church to want a husband.

The other problem is that what the congregation wants from the Man of God puts him under the Curse of the Law and curses his life, his wife, his children. The Church wants a husband; that's fine. She should realize that She is not designed to be complete without a husband. But if the church who **wants** a husband, not believing the Word, not believing that Christ will come decides to take a husband for Herself. There will be big trouble! She might say to her leader, **"Be our husband, and take away our approach."** Micah 4:1 reads, *Why do you cry aloud? Is there no king among you?*

In our example, we want Grandma to have the surgery, but the sin and crime committed to force it to happen, is not acceptable, and puts the bank robber under the Curse and into the penal system. Let me put it this way, just as the Church wants a husband, Grandma also wants the surgery. But there is a proper way to do everything. The Church **has** a Groom. He is Jesus. Grandma can have her surgery; she has insurance. Jesus is the *insurance* for the Church. Insurance is something that you might not be able to see as cash in the bank because the money that pays for things is not in your bank right now and it might not ever be in your bank, but insurance will come through. Jesus will come through as the Husband. The Church doesn't need to rob the pastor's wife of her husband to have one in the flesh. When the church's husband is for later, in the Spirit and for eternity.

Bride: You're not even ready yet, so what is your rush?

They did not *enter in* because of unbelief. If the Church does not have faith that She should, that God will perform His Word and Christ will return soon, She will fall into unbelief again. The Church wants a husband. Individually and collectively in this fatherless, husbandless society. And if they can get it from the man of God what they should be getting from Jesus--, if they can get it now, what they should be waiting for--, then by all means, too many go for it.

Church folks--, aren't we talking about the same folks who no longer wanted judges, they wanted a king? What is a husband but a king? Are we talking about the same folks who said we want what the world wants? Aren't we talking about people who want someone to look good for them or her and with him or her and stand head and shoulders above the rest? Are we talking about a spouse so that she can feel secure, protected, comforted, provided for, and special? Are we talking about people who have a sin nature to fornicate, to **not wait for marriage**, to not wait for the one? Are we talking about those folks?

Yep.

So, there he is, the one they love and adore--, their pastor. By trying to make him their "husband" they have soulishly and selfishly, put him under the **Curse of the Law** and wonder why he's so miserable, while they blame his perceived misery on his wife. He might be blaming his perceived misery on his wife! Surely if anyone of them were married to him, or their daughter, niece, Aunt, Mother, or grandmother, they could make that miserable pastor happy.

I know of at least one individual who has framed a picture of her pastor and has it on her desk at work. Her coworkers just recently found out that is not her husband.

If the pastor is not strong, he may accept this "love" from his congregation fornicating, as it were, spiritually, with the Lambs Bride. This causes the pastor to abide under the Curse. The people who put him there take care of him financially--, sometimes, and sometimes they don't. They don't want him to leave them-- *Don't go anywhere.* They say, *Don't travel. Don't spread the Word that the Lord has given you.* Yeah, they want him famous and popular, but they don't want him to go anywhere. *Just stick up under us and stay under the Curse by making **us** your spouse. Commit **spiritual** fornication and adultery with us.* They continue, *Because we want a husband **now**, We don't want to wait. We don't believe that we should wait.* They might as well say: ***We don't believe.***

Your pastor is not Christ. That church and every member in it belongs to God. Collectively, She is Jesus' Bride. Individually, each is the temple of the Holy Spirit.

Touch not God's *anointed.*

Fornication

The single people in any church are supposed to epitomize, personify, and model to the congregation for the Church is supposed to be like. Whole. One. A unit possessing their collective vessels (bodies) in honor. Singles, over and above any other group in the body should learn to be *satisfied singles*. Yet the singles are the ones who are trying to cling to and call on the pastor more and more. *Pastor, pastor. Pastor…*

While all this is going on, he forgot what God even called him to do. He just wants his flock to be *happy* and to *like* him, because if they like him then he can get them to do what he wants them to do when he asks. Does that mean that any fool thing they think of, he's supposed to do it? And does that mean any fool thing that he can think of, they're supposed to do it?

No and no. That's not what God said.

Just as you cannot allow Her to fornicate, you also cannot fornicate with the Church. The Bride of Christ can never be the bride or girlfriend of another.

The Church prophetically, is married to Jesus. In the Book of John, we learned that the woman at the well who should have been drawing out living water had five husbands already and was shacked up with the 6th man. Six is the number of man. She had been through five *religions* or denominations and was in her sixth, and still hadn't reached perfection. **Let the church hear what the Spirit is saying.** This passage is about the idolatry of the Church. This Woman *is* the Church—She's on her 6th one; instead of looking for God or toward God, She was looking toward man or man-made religions in a futile attempt to reach God. **God's way will reach man**; His arms are not too short, like ours. He can always reach us, but even if we try to build a tower, we cannot reach Him in the flesh.

This is God's Body. Touch, not inappropriately.

Perversions

Today's Church dangerously allow sex perversions in the name of Grace. Perverse souls will not enter into the Kingdom, so if these people are not being embraced for deliverance and conversion, then the embrace will connect the Church with the sin and She will not be adorned, beautiful, and blemish-free.

Clearly stated more than once in the Bible is that homosexuality is an abomination to God. Clearly understood that if a man expects to meet, date, marry a woman, it can't be a man. God is not mocked. I've seen churches with great choirs and praise teams collecting, as it were, those trapped in sin, not ministering to them, just collecting them as if somebody else is going to come and trouble the water, so they can be delivered. Deliverance is the children's bread. Pastor, if you're not called to deliver a sin sick soul from whatever malady, then invite a guest prophet or preacher in to minister Deliverance to your people. Deep rooted sin won't suddenly drop off because you're *nice* to somebody offering what you call Grace and letting them sing a solo on Sunday morning. Glory to God, for those who want deliverance from the things that oppress them if they have come into a church, it's usually to be set free, but not always. Some are on assignment; some are looking for dates. The Church should have the power to minister to everyone in the church and to set them free.

Jude 23 tells us to snatch such from the fires of Hell. *Snatch* is a one-time motion designed to move the person from harm's way immediately. *Snatching* does not take 3, 5, 7, or ten years of "fellowship" before the sinner falls drastically into all sin, even while in the church, then decides to try to live holy of his or her own volition. *Snatching* does not mean befriending until the sinner is on death's door, waiting until they want to repent. Repeating, snatching is a onetime action that pulls the sinner from the flames of hell, so the devil won't char boil him or her and *have it his way*.

I'm rather certain that even though Jesus dined with prostitutes and sinners, there was a conversion made in His presence. If your *presence* doesn't have that (or any) power because you are not *sent* there, then going there under the excuse of witnessing will not help the Church and its reputation, either in the world or, more importantly to God.

Snatch such a person implies a speed and quickness in the action, hating even the flesh-stained clothes they are wearing.

Today's Church has to be wary of those *sent* on evangelistic or deliverance assignments. Today's shepherd has to make sure those sent on assignment do not pervert the church over which he has oversight, as in the natural a woman with a "reputation" is not someone that a normal person would want to marry.

If the Church became chronically defiled with sin, Her reputation would precede Her, and she would not please the Lord. Christ, the unmarried Bachelor will not marry that *Woman* anyway, ready or not. The Bride of Christ, the Church is a Woman.

and in that day seven women will take hold of one man, saying we will eat our own bread. And where I own apparel only let us be called by thy name. To take away our approach, (Isaiah 4:1)

Churchzillas

I believe that Seven Women of which Isaiah speaks are saying something such as, *"Let us be called by your name so we can **say** we have a God, we can **say** we have a religion. We can say we have a purpose, a destiny or future, so we won't be looked upon as heathens or helpless people who have no God. Give us a **name** to put over our door, so we will know what to **call ourselves**, so we will know what to call our **denomination**."* Further, I believe they are saying, *"We will eat what we want, and we will dress how we want, but we need to take a name to take away the shame of not having a man--, **spiritually** speaking, not having a "religion" or a denomination."*

That is exactly what the Church has done in many instances, even today. She eats whatever She wants, whatever seems pleasing to Her, which is not always the Word of Truth. She wears whatever She likes. Isn't this all reminiscent of a child or a teenager? One of my numerous nieces, as a teen, for nearly three years would only eat cornbread, French fries, and string beans. Any of you have children know that at some point they do not like any item of clothing that you choose for them, but little ones want to dress themselves and the bigger ones want to choose what they will wear at the mall, and they expect you to pay for it. Those children are in essence saying to their parents, *"We will do, eat, say, and wear whatever we want. But just **say** you are our parents."*

How childish.

Then how childish the Church.

Churches are in the throes of narcissism, ego tripping and self-absorption; image is everything. They are world entangled. They lead an image-driven life. It's all about what it looks like, not so much what it really is. And is there any doctrinal truth in the foundation of what is believed? It's as though they are saying, *"We just need a name so we can get a 501C3 tax exempt nonprofit status. We just need a name so we will know what we are called, so we will know what convention to go to once a year. We just need a name so we will know which paraphernalia to buy from the Christian bookstore."* Like Isaiah's Prophecy, *"We're really going to do whatever we want, but just let us **use** your name."*

Anything improperly used is abused, according to Dr. Myles Munroe. He says, "The Church's purpose is to worship and glorify God in the Earth and to fulfill the Great Commission. If She's not doing that, then She is abusing power, authority, and people".

The Church has not been properly taught, even though Word Churches started 30 or so years ago. This could be why Churchzilla behaves as She does; She hasn't been taught.

She may be unteachable. Because of Her pride she may have become hard-headed and unteachable.

As a person with the anointing of a teacher, I also know that being able to teach is part of the gift of teaching, being able to reach souls and minds where they are, then stretch and strengthen them and lead them to new levels is part of the gifting. Another part of the dynamic belongs to the hearer who sits under good teaching. It causes the hearer to begin to thirst and hunger for more good teaching, it stimulates the mind and spirit and causes the hearer to become a seeker of knowledge, information, and Wisdom. It's like a Lay's potato chip; *you can't eat just one*. Just one snippet of God-knowledge, or revelation that reaches the place of a man's understanding causes a hunger for more. The preacher-teacher has been given an anointing to blast away unteachable-ness. However, if week after week, there's been nothing worthy taught, even if the member continues to come to church, after a while, the congregant will turn off their spiritual listening ears.

Churchzilla has not been loved. The Lord disciplines, chastises, corrects, and prunes those whom He loves. Grace-only pastors who have no accountability themselves and require none of their parishioners dole out no correction or discipline--, Grace only, and that's not good.

We should not provoke our children to wrath. Not teaching our children is provocation. It is provocation in the sense that they **must** be corrected later and sometimes by very inconvenient methods such as the penal system. This provokes them to anger because they don't understand why isn't everyone treating them as they're nice, pushover parents who let them get away with everything?

The same is true of church. What a shame to go to a new church or get a new pastor only to find out that you haven't been taught properly or that you haven't been taught anything at all.

False love is not love at all.

Churchzilla has not been properly loved. She has not had anyone to love Her or demonstrate to her how to correctly love others. So, She has turned to self-love. Until a woman has had a father's love, she has not been properly prepared for marriage, in the natural or in the spirit. Self-Love is a breach in the covenant that God has made with man. We are made to worship God, so when we turn to self-love, we break fellowship with the Lord, and we break covenant.

Churchzilla's self-will, doing what feels good or what seems right in her own eyes. She has little to no manners, no home training. Many local congregations don't know their purpose, their spiritual gifts, have had no experience using them and do not know how they fit together with other believers. Some corporations have better order and unity than some churches, and that's a sad state of affairs.

Churchzilla worships Herself. She worships Her own image. **She has created Herself in Her own image**, and that scary. Frankenstein's Bride, the man-made bride, who is just as bad as Bridezilla, the self-made bride that wants to marry Christ. *Eww*! That will never happen. Frankenstein's Bride wasn't even fitly joined together, and Bridezilla is a flesh mess. The Church must be fitly joined and mature in the things of God.

Churchzilla worships Her worship. She loves Her singers, Her choirs, Her dancers, Her mimes. She chases worship projects and et cetera. She worships Her ministry, which should include mercy and missions and benevolence and the like, but she may be cold and uncompassionate. She's a narcissist and a narcissist can only love self. She is incapable of loving others. She's self-absorbed from morning to evening.

She's a self-willed and a spoiled brat. She may be ruthless in Her drive to have Her own way.

Her touted and perceived importance has caused this narcissism. She's gotten Her big head now and you can't tell Her anything, or teach Her much at all. Her itching ears are being scratched; it is all about Her. The daring preachers preach contemporary sermons in an appalling vernacular, which tickles Her ears as he talks about hip-hop and rap, and even cites the filthy lyrics from the pulpit. She giggles. She giggles, but she's not learning anything. It's just an echo of what She did last night, or a rehearsal for what She's going to do when She gets home anyway. And this daring preacher will not prepare the congregation for marriage to the Lamb.

This weak preacher who doesn't want to take too long on Sunday, who preaches the 12-minute or six-minute homily--, his congregation won't be prepared either. The lazy preacher who doesn't and won't study, his congregation will be ignorant and rejected by Christ. The self-appointed ain't-even-called to be a preacher, his congregation will be led in the opposite direction of Christ. These ineffective, defective, un*called* preachers are Churchzilla-makers, and nobody wants a Churchzilla.

Much like the Bridezillas and the natural that are usually unsaved and in emotional pain or have issues and don't know that they need to deal with them and much less *how* to deal with them. Churchzillas, in essence, terrorize people. They are often overbearing and insist on their own way. They want to **make** folks accept them.

The second and third Revelation epistles revealed that the Churches then were much like the Churches now. And of all ages, that is an intermingling of good and bad, and is full of workings of depravity as the fruits of a true faith. There is so much to commend, but quite as much to censure even 2000 years later. We are still not out of the woods, and there's much work to do in our individual churches that will comprise the collective Church. It's very serious and we can take a lesson from the Seven Churches of the Revelation who could not hold the ground of Christianity in Asia Minor, having it overrun with other religions who have proudly won secularism as a choice.

When God gives a land to a people, He expects them to hold onto it.

Worse, if She's not doing what She was purposed to do and told to do, She will be without a king, without a husband. She'll be an *old maid*. And I mean old--, more than 2000 years old. Imagine. if when you were a kid, your mom told you to go to your room and clean it and don't come out until you finish. The Church has had more than 2000 years to accomplish this task, has She failed, after all that time?

This is not good.

...take away our reproach. Isaiah 4:1c

The Old Maids

Five of the ten virgins from the New Testament parable will not get married. Imagine that, and they're virgins. In the natural those gals would complain that they never had any fun, didn't go out and party like all their contemporaries. They never enjoyed life or had anything and still didn't have anything to look forward to. Only two of the Seven Churches as they were, were promised a name change. Philadelphia and Smyrna, and that's less than 30%.

Old Maids is not just a card game. The *old maids* who won't get married like Sardis, which today has no church and no city; it is only something old for archaeologists to study. The unprepared Churches will be rejected and made into *old maids*. Everyone that cries, *"Lord, Lord",* will not be saved.

So, the Church has created *Herself* in Her own image according to what pleases Her. Of the so-called pastors who have preached to Her, from them she has accepted pieces and parts of any and everything, including Pagan religions, *old wives' tales* and traditions. She has done with seems right in Her own eyes. Some of it is rebellion. She has, while even sitting under a pastor, stepped out from under covering. Sometimes is the ineffectiveness of the pastor himself. It does not matter who is to blame, but it does matter if She is prepared when the Righteous Judge steps on the scene to choose His collective Bride.

The Gospel must be preached everywhere before the Lord's return. So, these preachers and teachers, missionaries, apostles and evangelists better get serious. That's all of us, you know.

Today's Church believes that She looks pretty good, even though She may be living Her image-driven life, She enjoys many of the comforts of the world. She dresses as She pleases. She's got plenty to eat. She comes and goes as She pleases. Some Members are still members on the CME plan; they come to church on Christmas, Mother's Day, and Easter. She's not that uncomfortable during the preaching event; most preachers won't offend her, so no one makes Her give. Barna states that less than 20% of the so-called Churches tithe. She does what she wants pretty much and still believes that she's fine. She may not have given any thought to this marriage to the Lamb thing, since most preachers don't even preach it. Mostly, they talk about whether or not individuals are going to Heaven. The collective vision and purpose of being a pastor seems to escape many preaching and teaching events.

Is She going to Heaven? Maybe.

Will She be married to the Lamb? That's not my call, but I will now give a composite of the Seven Churches of the Apocalypse to get a snapshot of the collective Church of Asia Minor of 2000 years ago. These are the things that the Church of Ephesus, Smyrna, Pergamos, Thyatira, Sardis, Philadelphia, and Laodicea brought to the prenuptial table when they were evaluated in the Book of the Revelation, respectively, the Church in Asia Minor was hardworking, persevering, couldn't tolerate wicked men, tested so-called apostles and prophets, and judged them by the Word. She endured hardships and hated the things that Christ hated, namely the Nicolaitanes.

She was rich.

She lived in Satan's culture, but she remained true, not denying the Lord.

She had faith, service, and perseverance, even escalated to do more at that time than when She first started.

There were still some among Her that were pure and could still wear white.

She had brotherly love. She had kept the Lord's Word and had not denied His Name. She had endured patiently, even in Her weakness.

Another Church was rich in the natural.

The aforementioned seven paragraphs speak of some pretty nice things about the Church collectively as one Woman. Those are good traits, but doesn't the Lord deserve more? These traits, even in combination, did not make up a *whole* Bride. It was good that each Church had its forte, but the goal is to become **whole** in the Kingdom. The mandate is without spot, blemish, wrinkle or any such thing.

Conversely, the bad things, the spots, blemishes, and wrinkles on those Seven Churches were as follows.

She had forsaken Her first love.

She had some Jews living among them who were of the synagogue of Satan.

She had some Nicolaitanes whom the Lord hates, living among them, and had teachers of Balaam living among them teaching sexual immorality and teaching the people to eat idol's food.

She had a reputation and a name of being alive, but they were dead.

I know the Church had Jews of the Synagogue of Satan among them.

She was passionless, neither hot nor cold. They were wretched, pitiful, poor, naked. They lacked passion,. They showed signs that they were on their way to being dead like the other dead church above.

No single person, no single church or the Church collectively can counteract their own shortcomings by being good.

Spots, blemishes, wrinkles in any such thing are the requirements. If the inspector can't put the ***inspected by*** tag on that article of clothing in a factory, for example, then it must be rejected. This article may be sold as an overrun, or imperfect. It may be given away to charity, it may be burned. Either way, it will not enjoy the life that the perfect, unblemished, unwrinkled items enjoy. In the same way, the wanna-be-bride that can't make the cut will **not** be married. Christ will not just marry Her anyway. She will become an *old maid*. Christ hasn't rejected Her because She's old, they're all old, more than 2000 years old.

It is no coincidence that the pastor performs the weddings, binding grooms with brides. He is also the one to make the hook up between the Church and Christ by making people ready without spot, blemish, wrinkle, or any such thing. Are people prepared for the Lord? If he is not making the Church ready for Christ while at the same time both ministering to their needs in the natural and teaching them how to live victoriously, then he is slack.

Christ will not marry **Churchzilla**. No need for these wannabe-brides to feel jilted. There's been plenty of warning He will not stand like a wounded pup spouting, *"The invitations have already been sent,"* or *"I hope she changes,"* or, *"The guests have already arrived."* As evidenced by the Book of the Apocalypse, Revelation, He will **not** marry that woman or any woman with spot, blemish, defect, wrinkle, and *issues* that should have been and could have been worked out in the Earth. It just ain't happening.

Churchzilla's image, attitude and behavior are all deal-breakers. She will **not** be married. She will be an *old maid*, full of the shame, reproach, and damnation to eternal death. The desolation of two Churches in their respective cities were two of the Seven Churches. Shouldn't that be evidence enough, that God is not playing games, cards, or with people or churches. If changes are not made, some will not *enter in*to marriage with the Lamb. And there will be *old maids*.

For as a young man marrieth a young virgin, so shall thy sons marry thee; and as the bridegroom rejoiceth over the bride, so shall thy God rejoice over thee,
(Isaiah, 62:5).

Adorning the Bride

The **Bachelor**, still looking good, but still looking, 2000 years later. He's still looking and will soon return. He who finds a wife finds a good thing and obtains favor from the Lord. What might a Good Wife for the Lamb look like?

I'm not the Lord's matchmaker, but I found a woman and I'd like to tell you about her. She delights in his kisses, his smell, his Name, even where He works, she delights in intimacy with him. She knows her own shortcomings in the natural. For instance, that she is dark, but that she is lovely. She has neglected her own vineyards, but she has love for her brothers and has preferred them, tending to their vines. She's taking care of others.

She listens to the one she loves. She listens. He listens to her. They have excellent communication. They have mutual love. He is as into her as she is into him. She brags on Him. She fasts. She is enamored of Him, so much so that sometimes she forgets to eat.

She's endured hardship. She's even been beaten up in the streets while out looking for Him.

Their time of intimacy is guarded by 60 soldiers.

She knows Him, describing Him in great detail. She exhibits great passion. He knows her in great detail. He selected and elected her. He chose her out of 60 Queens, 80 concubines and numerous numbered virgins. One, she's the one. He is all into her.

And she is all into Him.

My lover's mine and I am His.

They are friends. It is not all about romantic love or lust. This is my Beloved and this is my Friend.

She did not leave her first love. She adored Him from the beginning, and told everyone about Him. She allowed Him to leave because it was the season of work And he had to go to work. That was synonymous with the Jewish betrothal of not knowing when the groom would return. She got up and went looking for Him, which may not be ladylike, but the Church should be *God chasers*.

She was faithful in tribulations, and even got beat up by the guards in the streets. She loved Him in spite of the fact that Her brothers didn't want her to. She wanted to be where He was to spend time with Him. His work was important to her.

I have just presented the **Shulamite woman**.

The Church is betrothed to be married to Christ, and She needs to be prepared, able, even exemplifying Her ability to *be* a wife. A Wife is called be a *helper*. She should be able to minister to not only Christ in praise and worship and offerings and blessings and in eulogy and coming under His mission, which is ministering to a sin sick world, redeeming them back to the Father.

His mission is reconciliation and redemption.

His mission is healing.

His mission is love.

His mission is deliverance and setting the captives free.

His mission is comfort.

His mission is the little children.

His mission is feeding the hungry, giving drink to the thirsty.

His mission is evangelism.

His mission is shepherding.

His mission is conversion.

His mission is to restore order and authority to mankind.

Jesus said, *If you've done it unto the least of these, you've done it unto Me.* As the Church prepares to become the Bride of Christ, She adorns Herself with the ability to help Him, assist Him in making sure the above-mentioned things happen in the Earth realm. As She does any of these acts of ministry unto the least in the Earth, She's preparing Herself, beautifying Herself and lighting Her lamp.

Ten virgins should have trimmed their lamps as they awaited the Bride Groom. Ten, the number of completion and completeness and the number of fullness. The Church should have completely prepared, practiced, exercised, and even rehearsed to fulfill its role as Wife to the Bridegroom when He returns for His glorious Church.

Do not miss this: She, the Church must be a virgin. That means that she is not covenanted or cavorted with any others. She is not falling into sexual or other covenants in idolatry, or she will not be considered a virgin.

The Church should be able to do any and all of that as She trims Her lamps. Her lamps should be set out for the world to see. The light of these lamps is to draw the world in from its darkness. Her lamps light the path and make the way for feet that must travel from hell to heaven. The Church's lamps must be trimmed and lit. The entrance of the Word of God gives light.

At the same time, this Woman, this Church, should be ministering to Jesus as the Body of Christ worshipping, praising, ministering, and bringing gifts and offerings. Her husband is known by the elders in the gates because She has told the world about Him.

And all the while, Jesus is treating the Church as a man should treat His wife, washing Her with the washing of the water of the Word, ministering to her needs, making provision for Her. Blessing Her, keeping Her, ultimately presenting Her to the Father without spot, stain, wrinkle, blemish or any such thing which is the exact thing a man should be doing in the natural with his natural wife.

A picture in a mirror, the spiritual and the natural. A man and his wife, the Christ in His Church.

If She is to be a *helpmate*, then She has to prepare Herself. She has to be properly trained. She could be *all that* the Good Book says, but that will take a proper spiritual father, proper role modeling and mentoring. That will take proper leadership.

The letters to the Seven Churches were all addressed to the Angel, the pastor who should be exhibiting proper leadership in each Church. In Jewish terms, that is, **sheliyach tsiyhuwr**, and it refers to the appointed messenger of the congregation that Angel Pastor had the job to lead, teach, and pray for and over in that Assembly. The modern cry should be, *"To your knees, O preachers, to your knees!"*

Impartation by the spiritual leader happens on more than one level. Involuntary, conscious, and unconscious. **Voluntary transfer** is when a leader may choose to have a consecration service where he may lay hands on all the ministers or everyone for that matter, as he imparts of his spirit, just as those under Moses. This is so they could help Moses judge when he was overwhelmed with the issues of the people, just as when Saul was turned into another man after spending time in the presence of the prophets.

Then there is the **involuntary transfer**, where everyone who sits under a man partakes of his grace. Do as I say and not as I do, doesn't work in the natural, and it definitely doesn't work in the church. Children are especially impressionable, and they will do and say what they hear and see, whether you want them to or not.

This entire treatise has been to prove that without proper teaching, no one can learn anything. Without proper teaching, even those who have promises may not be prepared to receive them. Those who have vision may not be able to fulfill them if they are not properly taught. This responsibility falls on the shepherd of the local assembly to teach the congregants, to unify them and to prepare them to become part of the collective Church that would be prepared and pleasing to the Lamb.

I've cried out in this writing that a preacher is not an entertainer. He's not merely a friend. He should not be a hireling, who works only for money, or for himself. He must be *called*. He must either know how to teach, for example, if he is gifted as an evangelist. Or he must know how to use the teachers that the Lord places in the local congregation and the Body in general to make sure the people are prepared and not ignorant.

The same judgments of approximately 2000 years ago in Asia Minor may still apply today, and that's sad. Have we learned nothing? Has the Church even read those Apocalyptic judgments in the Book of the Revelation? Have their pastors expounded on those letters crying out for unity, change, growth, maturity, passion, rightly dividing the Word, hard work, and perseverance? Have they cried out, hating what God hates, while invoking faith, service, doing good works, keeping the Lord's Word, not denying His Name, loving one another and maintaining purity to continue in holiness?

Have the preachers and pastors charged the slack Church that has forgotten Her first love, or the one who has tolerated sexual immorality, or eaten that which pertains to idols or tolerated the teachings of Jezebel? Have the pastors charged Her who is dead even though She carries the *name* of the Lord, which should indicate that She is alive? Have they called out the one that's passionless, wretched, blind, naked, poor, and pitiful?

If no preacher or pastor has *called* you to Biblical literacy, let this book do so now. Read your Bible, learn your Bible. Spend time in prayer and meditation talking to the Lord about what the passages mean. Be a member of a good teaching congregation and ask questions.

Be ready for marriage to the Lamb, be in a congregation that is all about being ready for marriage to the Lamb.

Focus on the big picture rather than the little things. I know a man who misses **all** of praise and worship nearly every Sunday for choosing, selecting, organizing, matching, and putting together what he will wear to church. I mentioned that he misses praise and worship to a friend of mine, and she countered with, *"No he's not. The clothes, shoes and accessories **are** his praise and worship.* How right she is. His intimacy is with his items of apparel, not with the Lord.

Naked he came into the world and naked is how he will leave. There's no outfit that will get him into Heaven.

Don't be like that guy; caught up in the natural when there is a whole spiritual world that we need to learn about, know about and maneuver through, even though it seems to be invisible to us. Walk by the Spirit and you will not fulfill the lusts of the flesh.

By proper teaching, the Church is uplifted. She is instructed, She is disciplined. She is exhorted. She is encouraged. She is convicted. She's forgiven. She's disciplined. She's given hope. She's corrected. She could find herself in the Word. She's unified by the Word. She's washed by the washing by the water of the Word.

She puts off the *old man* and she puts on the new man, becoming a **new creation.**

She grows up, She matures.

She learns to love.

She puts on Grace and compassion.

She meets Jesus.

She gets to know Him; she learns of Him and about Him.

She courts Her *Beloved.*

She becomes hidden in Him.

She becomes adorned for Her groom.

...the Lord will wash away the filth of the women of Zion. He will cleanse the blood stains from Jerusalem by spirit of judgment and a spirit of fire. (Isaiah 4:4 NIV)

Thank God for Grace and Mercy

Thank God for the Blood of Jesus.

As a dentist, today I performed three surgical dental extractions on a young lady. I packed the extraction sites with special surgical materials and gave her both verbal and written instructions on how to care for the extraction areas for the next few days. Of course, it's only been a few hours since she left my office, and she's already having problems because she is not following the instructions. She's doing what she thinks or *feels* to do or what her mother or grandmother (who were not present) tells her. She just admitted to me, over the telephone, that she has already rinsed her mouth, even though we expressly told her not to do that for 24 hours. That is an explicit no-no. And anyone of you who've ever had dry socket knows exactly what I'm talking about. If this young lady has dislodged the surgical packing and her blood clot, then she is in for some real pain. I do pray that she hasn't.

Thank God for our blood, for the healing power and nature of it. It is mysterious and miraculous the things that our own blood does for us. In the case of these extractions or any dental extractions, the presence of blood forms a clot and protects the extraction site from dry socket. The presence of the blood forms a matrix that begins the healing process to renew the area and begin the formation of new bone where the tooth, or teeth were extracted.

We are fearfully and wonderfully made. Thank God for our blood.

Thank God all the more for the Blood of Jesus to close and heal the negative spaces and places in our lives. If it were not for His Blood, we'd be *exposed* and in pain all the time. We'd never heal. But not for the Blood of Jesus, none of us could come to God, repent, be forgiven, or have our sins washed away. God sees us through the Blood of His Son, and thereby calls us *sons*.

The Blood of Jesus cleanses our blood, saves the blood, purifies the blood, protects the blood, heals the blood, provides redemption, atonement, justification, and a clear conscience. The Blood cleanses the blood, designates us as being in the family of God and brings peace.

The Lord's letters to the Seven Women, the Seven Churches are actually judgments that outline the breaches in the prenuptial agreement. The Woman (Church) is to prepare Herself with the appointed leadership, which is the Angel of that Assembly who outlines the breaches of each of the Churches. Some say that these are sentences from the Judge of the Churches, as they undergo inspection and decision. When finished, these churches, and hence the Church, shall be presented to Christ, and He will contemplate from the Judgment Seat.

Still, the Lord does not issue a death edict or warrant or arrest with a prison term; He offers Grace.

Were it not for the Lord's Grace and Mercy, and the Blood, the Church at Ephesus would not have had the opportunity to repent, and the Lord's Presence would have been removed from that place. Also, without the Lord's Grace and Mercy, Ephesus would not have been given the opportunity to eat of the Tree of Life in the Paradise of God.

Were it not for the Lord's Grace and Mercy the Church at Smyrna would not have been able to endure the 10 days of persecution that was forecasted for Her, and there would have been no crown of life for overcoming. There would have been no overcoming without the Blood.

Were it not for the Lord's Grace and Mercy and the Blood, the Church at Pergamos would not have had space to repent. They would have perished by the Sword of the Lord's mouth. They would not have earned, as overcomers, the hidden manna and the White

Stone with a New Name on it that no man knows except the person that receives it. Thank God for The Blood.

Were it not for the Lord's Grace and Mercy, and the Blood of Jesus, the Church at Thyatira would not have been able to repent, and to hold on until the Lord comes, and then be given an iron scepter to rule over the nations. They would not have been able to receive the Morning Star for overcoming.

Were it not for the Blood, for God's Grace and Mercy, the few of the Church at Sardis, who had not stained their clothes, would not be able to walk with the Lord. Had it not been for the Lord's Great Mercy, **all** their names would have been blotted out of the Book of Life, and the Lord would not have acknowledged them before His Father.

Were it not for the Lord's Grace and Mercy and the Blood, the Church at Philadelphia would not have been able to hold on, so that no one would take Her crown, she also would not have made Her a perpetual pillar in the Temple of God, never to leave the Lord's Temple. And on this pillar is written the name of God and the name of the City of God, the New Jerusalem, and also the Lord's New Name.

Were it not for the Lord's Grace and Mercy and the Blood, the Church at Laodicea would not have had the opportunity to repent and to open the door where the Lord stood and knocked. They would not have been offered to sit with the Lord on His Throne had it not been for Grace, Mercy, and the Blood of Jesus.

Except for Grace, Mercy, and the Blood of Jesus, you and the church in your city would have no time for repentance and overcoming. There'd be no precious promises such as a new name and marriage to the Lamb.

Without the Blood, without Grace and Mercy, none of us individually, and no local assembly in the collective Church would have any hope of Eternal Life.

I wed thee forever. Not for now.
Not for the sham of Earth's brief years.
I wed thee for the life beyond the tears.
Beyond the heart pain and the clouded brow.
Love knows no grave, and it will guide us dear
When life's spent candles flutter and burn low.

Anderson Baten

Dear Reader

Thank you for acquiring, reading, and sharing this book. The Holy Spirit inspired me greatly in its creation and I pray that that you can say the same in reading it.

God bless you,

In the Name of Jesus,

Amen.

Dr. Marlene Miles

Prayer books by this author

While most books by this author have prayer points either throughout the book or at the end, there are some books that are **only** prayers. You just open up the book and pray. They are listed below:

Prayers Against Barrenness: *For Success in Business and Life*

Fruit of the Womb: *Prayers Against Barrenness*

Beauty Curses, *Warfare Prayers Against*
https://a.co/d/5Xlc20M

Courts of Marriage: Prayers for Marriage in the Courts of Heaven *(prayerbook)* https://a.co/d/cNAdgAq

Courtroom Warfare @ Midnight *(prayerbook)*
https://a.co/d/5fc7Qdp

Demonic Cobwebs *(prayerbook)* https://a.co/d/fp9Oa2H

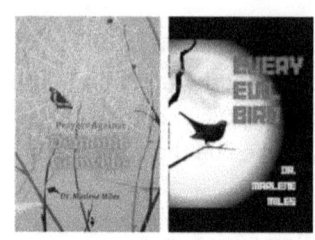

Every Evil Bird https://a.co/d/hF1kh1O

Every Evil Arrow https://a.co/d/afgRkiA

Gates of Thanksgiving

Spirits of Death & the Grave, Pass Over Me and My House https://a.co/d/dS4ewyr

*Please note that my name is spelled incorrectly on amazon, but not on the book.

Throne of Grace: Courtroom Prayer

https://a.co/d/fNMxcM9

Warfare Prayer Against Poverty
https://a.co/d/bZ61lYu

Other books by this author
Abundance of Jesus, *The*

AK: *The Adventures of the Agape Kid*

AMONG SOME THIEVES

Ancestral Powers https://a.co/d/9prTyFf

Backstabbers https://a.co/d/gi8iBxf

Barrenness, *Prayers Against* https://a.co/d/feUltIs

Battlefield of Marriage, *The*

Beware of the Dog: *Prayers Against Dogs in the Dream*

Blindsided: *Has the Old Man Bewitched You?*
https://a.co/d/5O2fLLR

Break Free from Collective Captivity

Caged Life https://a.co/d/0eKxbU9H

Casting Down Imaginations https://a.co/d/1UxlLqa

Churchcraft: Witchcraft In the Church

Churchzilla, The Wanna-Be, Supposed-to-be Bride of Christ

Curses of Blind Men

Demonic Cobwebs (prayerbook)

Demonic Time Bombs

Demons Hate Questions (mini book)

Devil Loves Trauma, *The*

Devil Weapons: Unforgiveness, Bitterness,...

The Devourers: *Thieves of Darkness 2*

Do Not Swear by the Moon

Don't Refuse Me, Lord (4 book series)
https://a.co/d/idP34LG

Dream Defilement

The Emptiers: *Thieves of Darkness, 1*
https://a.co/d/5I4n5mc

Every Evil Arrow https://a.co/d/afgRkiA

Evil Touch https://a.co/d/gSGGpS1

Failed Assignment https://a.co/d/3CXtjZY

Fantasy Spirit Spouse https://a.co/d/hW7oYbX

FAT Demons (The): *Breaking Demonic Curses*

The Fold (5-book series)
- The Fold (Book 1)
- Name Your Seed (Book 2)
- The Poor Attitudes of Money (3)
- Do Not Orphan Your Seed (4)
- For the Sake of the Gospel (5)
- My Sowing Journal

Gang Ups: *Touch Not God's Anointed*

got HEALING? Verses for Life

got LOVE? Verses for Life

got HOPE? Verses for Life

got money? https://a.co/d/g2av41N

Has My Soul Been Sold?

How to Dental Assist

How to Dental Assist2: Be Productive, Not Wasteful

I Take It Back

Legacy

Let Me Have A Dollar's Worth
https://a.co/d/h8F8XgE

Level the Playing Field
https://www.youtube.com/watch?v=BfF-TX1EWNQ

Living for the NOW of God

Lose My Location https://a.co/d/crD6mV9

Love Breaks Your Heart

Man Safari, *The* (mini book from The Wilderness Romance)

Marriage Ed. Rules of Engagement & Marriage

Made Perfect in Love

Money Hunters: Beware of Those

Money on the Altar https://a.co/d/4EqJ2Nr

Mulberry Tree https://a.co/d/9nR9rRb

Motherboard (The) - *Soul Prosperity Series*

Name Your Seed

Occupy: *Until I Return*

Plantation Souls

Players Gonna Play

Power Money: Nine Times the Tithe
https://a.co/d/gRt41gy

Powers Above

Repent of Visiting Evil Altars https://a.co/d/3n3Zjwx

The Robe, *Part 1, The Lessons of Joseph*

The Robe, *The Lessons of Joseph* Part II,

Seasons of Grief

Seasons of Waiting

Seasons of War

Second Marriage, Third--, *Any Marriage*

https://a.co/d/6m6GN4N

Sift You Like Wheat

Six Men Short: What Has Happened to all the Men?

Son https://a.co/d/09mIThSg

Soul Prosperity, Soul Prosperity Series Bk 3 https://a.co/d/5p8YvCN

Souls Captivity, Soul Prosperity Series Book 2

The Spirit of Poverty

StarStruck

SUNBLOCK

The Swallowers: Thieves of Darkness, Book 3

Take It Back

This Is NOT That: How to Keep Demons from Coming at You

Time Is of the Essence

Too Many Wives: *Why You Have Lady Problems*

Tormenting Spirits https://a.co/d/dAogEJf

Toxic Souls

Triangular Power *(series)*

- Powers Above
- SUNBLOCK
- Do Not Swear by the Moon
- STARSTRUCK

Unbreak My Heart: *Don't Let Me Die* Uncontested Doom

Unguarded Hours, *The*

Unseen Life, *The* https://a.co/d/0drZ5Ll

Upgrade: How to Get Out of Survival Mode (and two more titles):

- Toxic Souls (Book 2 of series)
- Legacy (Book 3 of series)

WTH? Get Me Out of This Hell

The Wasters: *Thieves of Darkness,* Bk 2
https://a.co/d/bUvI9Jo

What Have You to Declare? What Do You Have With You from Where You've Been?

When I Was A Child, *I Prayed As a Child*

When the Devourer is Rebuked

https://a.co/d/1HVv8oq

The Wilderness Romance *(series)* This series is about conducting a Godly relationship and marriage with someone who is a Wilderness person. It is about how to recognize it and navigate through it. These books are about how not to get caught up in such.

- *The Social Wilderness*
- *The Sexual Wilderness*
- *The Spiritual Wilderness*

Other Series
Matters of the Heart series

Made Perfect in Love https://a.co/d/70MQW3O

Love Breaks Your Heart https://a.co/d/4KvuQLZ

Unbreak My Heart https://a.co/d/84ceZ6M

Broken Spirits & Dry Bones https://a.co/d/e6iedNP

The Fold (a series on Godly finances)

https://a.co/d/4hz3unj

Soul Prosperity Series https://a.co/d/bz2M42q

Spirit Spouse books

https://a.co/d/9VehDSo

https://a.co/d/97sKOwm

Thieves of Darkness series
https://a.co/d/b07c8Ms

Triangular Powers https://a.co/d/aUCjAWC

Upgrade (series) *How to Get Out of Survival Mode*
https://a.co/d/aTERhXO

www.ingramcontent.com/pod-product-compliance
Lightning Source LLC
Chambersburg PA
CBHW070200100426
42743CB00013B/2985